MAURICE KOGAN is Professor of Government and
Social Administration and Head of the Department
of Government at Brunel University. He was an
administrator in the Department of Education and
Science from 1953 to 1967 and Secretary to the
Plowden Committee on Primary Education from 1963
to 1966. He was Director of the Hospital Organisation
Research Unit at Brunel University from 1967 to 1970.
He has been a member of the Houghton Committee
on Teachers' Salaries, of the Davies Committee on
Hospital Complaints Procedure, an adviser to the
House of Commons Committee investigating policy-
making in the DES, an examiner and consultant to
the OECD, and the Race Relations Board's assessor
on the Ealing bussing issue.

Political Issues of Modern Britain
Editors: Bernard Crick and Patrick Seyd

The Politics of Educational Change

MAURICE KOGAN

Fontana/Collins

Published by Fontana 1978
Copyright © Maurice Kogan 1978

Made and printed in Great Britain by
William Collins Sons & Co. Ltd, Glasgow

The Politics of Educational Change is published in
hardback by Manchester University Press

Contents

Editors' Preface

This new series aims to put into the hands of the intelligent general reader concise and authoritative accounts of the major issues of British politics today.

Writing on politics has often suffered from being either strident polemic or ephemeral journalism or else from being academic monographs too technical or theoretical for the general reader. This series hopes to fill an important gap—for it is more difficult to find reliable accounts of what happened ten or twenty years ago than fifty—by covering the issues which opinion polls and experts have judged to be the major issues of contemporary British politics.

We say 'issues' deliberately and not *problems*. Perhaps, indeed, beneath all these explicit issues, election slogans, public worries and press campaigns, there are fundamental and implicit economic and social problems. Theories, whether Marxist or Capitalist, are not lacking to explain them all and to put them all in a 'correct theoretical perspective'. Our aim is more modest and precise: to remedy the lack of books that give accounts of those concerns which might reflect forces more fundamental, but will appear as concrete issues to ordinary people in everyday life. These books will be about politics and not political science.

Each book will cover three main topics: (i) a brief summary of the origins of the issue and fuller account of its history since the Second World War; (ii) an account of its institutional setting and of the pressure groups associated with the issues; and (iii) an account of what should be done and what is likely to happen. We ask each author to be as objective and as balanced as possible on the first two topics, but as polemical and as stimulating as he or she thinks fit in the third.

The series aims to achieve the same high standards of judgement but also of brevity that have been typical of the Fontana Modern Masters series. It aims to fulfil much the same function: both to be an introduction to the general reader and to be a way in which a specialist in one field can communicate with a specialist in another. If we may draw an analogy, we have briefed our authors to attempt that demanding but non-technical level of writing that is typical of the *Political Quarterly* at its best. Yet while the series is primarily intended for the general reader, students of history, politics, economics and social administration will find that the books fill a gap. They reflect a growing concern in the academic study of politics to look first at actual issues, rather than at institutions or methodologies.

If new editions are warranted, the complete books will, of course, be revised. But each time there is a reprint, we will ask the author to update the section on policy, on what is to be done. Thus each reprint will be topical while the edition places the issue in a deeper historical and institutional setting. We hope that this novel feature of the series will help it to be a contribution to what Walter Bagehot once hoped for from Parliamentary debates, 'the political education of mankind'. For that education seems at the moment so often to suffer from books which are a strange mixture of abstract theory and instant polemic. Issues need studying in an historical context if we are to act sensibly and effectively; and act we must.

Bernard Crick
Patrick Seyd

Author's Foreword

I wish to acknowledge the considerable help received in writing this book. I was greatly helped in the formulation of ideas by my colleague, Mary Henkel, of the Department of Government, Brunel University. Professor Tony Becher, Helen Fraser, Godfrey Golzen, Philip Kogan, Professor John Rear and Patrick Seyd also gave me invaluable suggestions on both the content and structure of this work.

I am much indebted to Sally Marshall for the expert typing of successive drafts of this book.

Introduction

Education is an area where political activity is at present prominent. This was not always so. In the 1940s and 1950s, in spite of underlying tensions and conflicts, the appearance was of tranquil progress and consensus. No politician worth his salt could contemplate office in the Ministry of Education for long because it lacked the newsworthiness associated with, say, the Ministries of Transport or of Housing and Local Government (as they used to be called) or the Home Office, let alone the Treasury or Foreign Office. In local government, too, education until a decade or so ago seemed set in a cosy and bi-partisan consensus.

This began changing in the mid-1960s. The intellectuals and the egalitarians had been at work for some time and before long reactions began to be felt. The expansion of the system, the move away from elite higher education following the Robbins Report, the drive of successive Labour governments towards universal comprehensive secondary education, were accompanied by many other dramatic movements of sentiment and policy. Their flashpoints included the recurrent troubles at the University of Essex and the Polytechnic of North London, and at the LSE where student dissidents pushed down the gates and two members of staff were dismissed; the challenge by grammar school parents to the Enfield local education authority; the three Black Papers on education; the Tameside defiance of a Labour Secretary of State and his defeat in the courts; the William Tyndale Inquiry and the resulting dismissal of teachers; and James Callaghan's Yellow Book. These are episodes in continuous and thematic stories that not only reflect on the politics of educational change but also mirror changes in the total social and political scene within which education moves.

This book is an attempt to show why education is important and exciting as an area of politics, and why the issues that emerge from the schools and the colleges have a far wider significance than education itself. Almost all of the issues discussed here bear on the major problems of our times. We cannot consider the ways in which society provides education without involving the perennial issues of political philosophy: who will decide on behalf of society what collective action shall be taken, how the power of the decision-maker is made legitimate, and how far decisions are democratically made. This book thus tries to show how, in one field of social policy, fundamental value conflicts and institutional pressures work out within the political and administrative system.

The plan of this book is as follows. Chapter 1 argues that education is important in terms of its internal politics. Chapters 2 and 3 describe some of the main substantive issues as they emerged and changed between 1945 and 1976. Chapters 4 to 8 show how education is social policy at large and is related to many of the current issues of politics and governance; these chapters also provide an account of the way in which the public system is required to be accountable and efficient yet sensitive to the demands of teacher professionalism, of trade union and client militancy, to the pressure from interest groups, and to the growing demands of consumerism and of participation. Chapter 10 analyses the main 'stake-holders' in education both within and outside the system. And finally I discuss those issues which might be important for the future.

If there is a single theme in this complicated story, it is that as changes in society have affected the expectations held of education, so the institutional fabric has found it difficult to contain the new forces pressing on it.

PART ONE

The Changing Context

Chapter 1 Why Education Is Political

Politics are those processes of discourse through which members of society seek to assert and ultimately reconcile their wishes. So those people who wish to make education non-political are either failing to understand that the purposes and procedures of education reflect what people want, or they are trying, perhaps unconsciously, to restrict the rights of fellow citizens to participate in decisions of deep and abiding importance to them. That is not to say that teaching should be politically biased. The fact that education brings into conflict so many different values makes it all the more important that pupils and students should be taught how to make their own choices.

Education, more than virtually any other social activity, is concerned with what *ought* to be rather than with what *is*. People become educated in order to promote changes in themselves or others. Some political actors, including Hitler and Lenin, hoped it would help them to change the world. All of the major religions have tried to use education to mould the morals and beliefs of the young. The changes desired in people are as various as the whole range of human desire and feeling, and may conflict with each other even within a single school or school system.

This emphasis on change is not contradicted by education's socialising aims. Education acts powerfully to train pupils to maintain an existing society, and to learn traditional skills or traditional attitudes. Those processes will themselves have changed the pupil into a member of society even if they have not encouraged him to change that society. The unit of discussion is, indeed, important. Individual and collective benefit are not the same thing. Nor are individual and collective change and development. Personal development may be compatible with the collective good. Quite often, however, they are in conflict.

Now education is a highly artificial business in the way that building houses, making roads, mending limbs, or defending one's family and property are not. There are innate desires to learn but education, as Europeans have universally come to understand it, involves schooling. Schooling causes societies to select and train adults to work as teachers who then spend most of their working lives in specially built and equipped school buildings where they work on tasks that might seem quite remote from ordinary living. Education is also artificial in the sense that a world without it is not only conceivable but possible; the world has been without organised education for most of its history.

It does not follow that the British citizen is wrong to spend so much of his total earnings on education. (About 3·2 per cent of the gross national product between the mid-1950s and -1960s went into it. By 1969 it was 6 per cent.) It does follow, however, that education is, more than most human activities, tied up with what people want to do and want to be rather than with what they must do and are compelled to be. As Julia Evetts has written in *The Sociology of Educational Ideas*, 'The changes in educational outlook parallel the changes which a nation undergoes in the course of its history.' Education is the most volatile of collective activities because it incorporates simultaneously so many aspirations. It contains the hope that man may change himself so as to be happier, more productive, a good neighbour; and the hope that social arrangements can incorporate both the best of the past and the promise of the future.

If, then, education responds to both social demands and individual aspirations, an examination of the main educational issues since 1945 will also entail an inquiry into some of the most important arguments about politics and society during that period.

Before looking in more detail at the issues with which educators and their children have been concerned, it will be well to be clear as to how controversies about educational policies are in fact controversies about man's individual and collective present and future wants.

Men wish to improve themselves, and for several reasons. The first is an innate desire to be more powerful and competent, and more in control of their own powers, for the sake of psychological comfort, of self-esteem. In that sense education is not artificial. It is a prime purpose of education to help a pupil to develop a sense of his own worth. This becomes particularly important in the middle years of secondary education when adolescence causes a surge of both optimism and uncertainty. Teaching a pupil to express himself clearly, to work competently, to attend to personal appearances and style, has an 'internal' or individual purpose as well as more socially instrumental or external purposes. This purpose of education, of giving pupils a sense of control over themselves, constitutes the *autonomy* or *freedom objectives* of education and relates quite closely to those of enabling pupils to be economically self-sufficient and to contribute their share to the formation of family or national wealth. Lack of economic self-sufficiency and an inability to contribute a share to the economy is a major component of lack of self-esteem and is thought to be 'stigmatising'. It is this *individual* objective of education that gives a fierce dynamic to education as a political force. Consider why parents become so anxious about patterns and choices of secondary education or the underlying conflicts in the William Tyndale School (see Chapters 4 and 7). The individual objective of education is that most strongly espoused by conservative policy-makers though their critics maintain that traditional systems are instrumental in creating elites and dutiful work-forces rather than enhancing personal freedom. It comes into conflict with the more collective aspirations of the left who see education as a way of causing social change and social cohesion.

These individual objectives of education are closely tied to the *social* objectives with which they may conflict.

Individuals need relationships with their family, peer groups, neighbourhood and work place if they are to function well as individuals. Interpersonal relationships, which are affected so deeply by a sense of self-esteem and adequacy, are learned socially, and the school is an important centre for such social learning. Social learning is an overt purpose of both primary and secondary education as both the Plowden and Newsom Reports (on primary and non-selective secondary education respectively) stated. It is also a traditional purpose of elite university education, as is obvious from the biographies of, for example, the leaders of the Bloomsbury group. This objective is pursued when nursery pupils learn to play in groups, primary pupils undertake projects together, and university students share seminars in which the conventions of social interplay have as much weight as rigorous demonstration of logic and power of argument.

In another and wider sense, education has social objectives. It transmits the dominant culture to new generations by inculcating norms of language such as those of 'received' English, or what Basil Bernstein (in 'Social Structure, Language and Learning'; *Educational Research* III, 3 June 1961) has called the elaborate code, imparted by education and society and by drawing attention to the accepted glories of the culture, such as the works of Shakespeare, eighteenth-century architecture and parliamentary modes of debate. Education also makes plain the acceptable standards of behaviour as laid down by law and by social convention: such as the correct behaviour between weak and strong, male and female, what attitudes towards personal property are acceptable, the need to make a contribution to society, to behave as a good democrat, and so on. In Britain this socialising process is often implicit. Most observers of the process consider it as part of an intuitive and natural consensus that exists among the great mass of reflective people in the country. Others reckon the socialising process to be part of a sort of slave owners' conspiracy to condition the mass of the people into doing what they are told. The reader might care to reflect on his own life history and see which account seems most true. But because education is held accountable for socialisation, its assumed failures to teach young people how to behave and how to work productively keep education central to the main discourse that constitutes politics.

The socialising process is implicit rather than overt in Britain. Its more explicit components, though hard to find, can be discovered in those curiously mummified residues of established religion known as 'religious education' and the 'act of worship', which are the only elements imposed by law on the British school curriculum. When they were written into the 1944 Education Act their authors must have had the same intentions as the Soviet educational planners who insist on the teaching of compulsory Marxism. That, too, we understand from Nigel Grant's authoritative *Soviet Education*, is a ritual 'like compulsory chapel', boring and unreal to most.

Indeed, the cases of religious education and the act of worship, as an example of compulsory socialisation from which unbelievers have to opt out, serve to remind us again of how education responds to social change. At one time, no statement of educational objectives could have omitted the intention of society to teach its young to believe in God and the consequential tenets of a true faith in Him.

This book does not, however, intend relating in detail the objectives of education, its institutions and its promises. The single major point made so far is that education and the schooling through which it is carried out are an artefact. Into that artefact is poured a wide range of human aspirations. Since human beings seek to be autonomous, free and self-respecting but are at the same time social, gregarious and potentially loving of others, and since they have to act collectively to defend, feed and house themselves through an economic system, it follows that education, too, offers a menu which has some sections à la carte but others consisting

19

of compulsory dishes. Social policy generally never fails to incorporate ambiguity or conflict about underlying values. The tension between social needs and private wants, the balance between freedom and control, between individual independence and collective effort, are present in discussions of who should get what in housing, health, social services, income reinforcement, or town planning. But because education is a desired artefact, rather than a self-evidently valued set of procedures, its content and form are far more open to dispute than other social provisions. Only perhaps, town planning which, too, expresses, or fails to express, what people want more than what they definitely need is reactive so much to fashion and to the range of human endeavours.

For these reasons education is political. It is volatile. It strongly reflects the often conflicting and wide-ranging preferences of a society which it also helps to sustain, improve, embellish and from which it draws resources. If politics are the way in which individuals assert their claims and have them reconciled with the claims of others, education reflects and clarifies and expresses those claims in the society, though it cannot of itself reconcile them.

Some of those claims changed radically between 1945 and 1976. There were dramatic changes in mass expectations to which the education system had to respond. The mechanisms and modes of those responses are the stuff of educational politics. In this book, the politics of educational change has two meanings. It is first the actions and belief of the main political parties. More important, however, the politics of educational change entails the study of changes in the total political and administrative system as reflected in, and precipitated by, changes in education.

Some changes were caused by and reflected by the political parties. But the reader will notice that the main political parties, as opposed to a few leading individuals within them, do not appear in this book as prominent actors in change. Both the political system of parliament and the party activities themselves, reflect, articulate and, to some extent, affect issues. They are not, however, prime movers although the main political parties both affected and were affected by the changes recorded in this book.

As we shall see later in the book, the Conservatives made education a component of the Opportunity State and thus have increasingly come into conflict with the Labour Party view, which took far longer to clarify, that education is an equalising force. Conservatives thus emphasised the individual objectives of education and concentrated on those social objectives which aim to produce an efficient workforce and a strong social fabric. Both of these assumptions explain their strong support for the expansion of higher education in the 1960s. The Labour Party first confused greater opportunity with greater equality but increasingly moved towards the 'strong' version of egalitarianism which argued for the creation of comprehensive schools. They hoped that the schools could heal the divisions of a class-ridden society. They have not yet resolved the concomitant problems of freedom of choice for those who want particular and privileged forms of education and who can either win it through competitive examination or pay for it.

These remain important issues of educational policy. But education in the last decade has moved beyond its traditional boundaries. The interplay between the larger political parties and the working out of solutions by the schools, colleges and public authorities are no longer the only sources of change. Important new attitudes and policies have started at the fringe of politics and have increasingly entered the main fabric of the system. The testing of authority has affected educational policies and interactions. The power of schooling and scholarship to refine and pass on knowledge as validated material, the assumption that schools and colleges are specialist institutions performing a professional function have been severely attacked by deschooling, free schools, and the radical student movements. Starting in part with fringe groups but also entering into the more serious framework of academic philosophy and sociology there is a strong critique which challenges the ability of the educational system to safeguard individual rights or those forms of the collective good which they regard as the most important.

In these changes of attitude we see symptoms of many of the moods and movements which affect British politics and social relations at large. The right to choose to work or not, the right to have access to social good without clear statements of responsibilities to society, the assumption that authority and institutions are no more legitimate than those who remain outside them, all of these 'fringe' assumptions can be found in all walks of life. Education is therefore not alone in responding to ideas from outside its own doors.

It is hoped that by now the reader will have accepted the general proposition that education reflects larger movements in society and in politics at large. This point will be confirmed by the story of changing expectations and policies which occupies Chapter 2.

Chapter 2 Expansion and Opportunity, 1944–64

BEFORE THE 1944 ACT: OPPORTUNITY FOR THE MINORITY

Education has always mattered to people. In the pre-war period and for some time afterwards, however, concern about it was mainly expressed by the liberal or radical elite outside the education service, and by the leaders of the education service itself. One of the important developments of the last thirty years is that a far larger number of people are now interested in education. In this, education is affected by the more general rise in consumer and voter expectations, and demands for participation.

Between 1918 and 1939 public expenditure on education was meagre and most people expected little from it. The Board of Education estimates in 1922–3 were £45 million. They rose to £51 million by 1938 which represented a 3 per cent increase at constant prices. So much of its important provision was available only to those who could afford it by paying for places at the universities or at the private schools, or in the fee-payers' places in grammar schools. Only a small and able minority of those without money could get through to the top levels of the system. Inasmuch as there was pressure for educational advance, it hardly came from the clients. In the 1970s not just middle-class parents but those from all groups are interested in comprehensive education or the retaining of grammar schools, and in what they and their children are getting from the schools. In the pre-1939 period, however, demands were mainly expressed by local authorities, by a minority of teachers, and by the small liberal intelligentsia which, through the Fabian Society and the Labour Party, advocated educational expansion. One of the most articulate of these was the great historian R. H.

Tawney who through his historical writing, through his own social tracts such as *Equality* (1931), through his membership of successive Board of Education Consultative Committees and his advocacy of adult education, made out both the general case and the specific proposals for equality. Apart, however, from a few leading seers the case for expansion and change was quite poorly supported. Indeed, at one point in the early 1920s when the British had one of their perennial purges of public expenditure, education had to defend itself against the cuts in salaries and other costs proposed by the Geddes Committee. As Brian Simon has so elegantly recounted, in *The Politics of Educational Reform 1920–40*, they intended raising the age of entry to six on the grounds that those starting at five did not seem to learn much more, and to save £8 million a year by providing only one teacher to fifty pupils in urban areas. Present-day radicals do not know what a real reactionary is like.

Most people before 1939 assumed that they would work from the age of fourteen. The 1939–45 war helped to change that. It gave many thousands of people their first glimpse of opportunity and of adult education. It shifted people out of their received notions of a fixed station in life. Many working-class people had never moved away from their home villages or town areas, even for holidays. They found themselves in the Middle East, in Europe, and treated as part of the nation's most important capability, the Armed Services. The armed forces, so hierarchical in format, could be democratic in some of their policies. Several who could never previously have aspired to it were given social status and personal resources through commissioned or non-commissioned rank. Immediately after the war many received a second chance to get into higher education. Some tens of thousands of returned warriors went into emergency training courses which staffed the schools during a period of great pressure and, incidentally, provided the schools with much of their leadership in the succeeding ten or twenty years. Those whose expectations were aroused may have been confusing social equality with individual opportunity. But during the war and the reconstruction period, of all the social services, education was seen as the agency through which people, pupils and parents would move towards participation in the benefits of a richer, fairer and more civilised society. Some, indeed, have said that the opportunities provided by war service directly affected immediate post-war politics and that the 1945 General Election was won for Labour by the Army Education Corps.

AN EXPANDING EDUCATION SERVICE, 1945–77

In the period 1945–77, the education service expanded at a phenomenal rate. As we shall see in the next chapter, education is a gigantic case study of how increased social and individual activity and commitment—more expenditure, more buildings, more people, more political support—do not necessarily lead to satisfaction and success.

Before looking at the main phases of expansion and expectation, deceleration and disappointment, however, the continuous process of expansion is conveniently recounted here. Expectations and politics changed but expansion occurred throughout our field until the mid-1970s.

The growth of the education system has been dominated by demographic change. Thus, the school population in England and Wales rose from six million in 1960 to nine million in 1977. This was partly the product of an increased child population, but also the result of conscious government policies, including the raising of the school leaving age from fourteen to fifteen in 1949 and to sixteen in 1972. It was also a reflection of public demand for education. We cannot compare GCE examination entries over the whole of our period because School and Higher School Certificates only gave way to GCE O and A levels in 1951, but, in 1952, 162,000 candidates made 830,000 O-level entries. By 1974, 810,000 candidates made 2,477,000 entries. A-level entries rose from 40,000 to 250,000 in the same period.

The university population grew from 68,000 in 1946 to 275,000 in 1977. Between 1952 and 1975, full-time further and higher education outside the universities grew from 70,000 to 400,000 students. In 1945, public educational expenditure was £144 million. By 1965 it was £1,115 million. In 1975–6, educational expenditure was nearly £6,000 million. It had thus tripled, at constant prices, between 1945 and 1965 and almost doubled again between 1963 and 1976.

Some indicators of educational growth are given in the table below:

Indicators of Educational Expansion, 1937–76
(England and Wales)
All figures are thousands

	1937/8	1946/7	1950/1	1964/5	1975/6
Full-time and full-time equivalent pupils in schools	5,599	5,100	5,985	7,181	9,254
Full-time and full-time equivalent teachers in schools	196	154	227	294	469
College of education, full-time equivalent students	10	18	23	70	88
University full-time and full-time equivalent students	39	68	69	105	223

Source: *Statistics of Education, 1975*, Vol. V: Finance and Awards; Table 1.1 (DES Annual Report).

The whole system thus expanded continuously, if by fits and starts, from the end of the 1939–45 war until the present time. But the expectations of and attitudes towards education were less continuous than its numbers and resources imply.

It is thus possible to divide the period into four overlapping stages. Between 1945 and 1964 the main promises of the 1944 Act were to be implemented. During that time there were few to doubt that increased education in an increasingly rich society would give everybody what they wanted. The higher education system was greatly expanded in accordance with the Conservatives' belief in opportunity and Labour's far more tentative and unclarified hopes for equality. And both parties associated more education with an expanded economy. This period, however, held the seeds of later conflict. For from 1963 to 1970 a different mood set in. Dissatisfaction with the redistributive power of the Welfare State within a mixed economy lent strength to Labour's drive towards comprehensive education and the creation of educational priority areas at the same time as the higher education system expanded and became a principal forum of social dissent. From 1970 to 1974 the Conservatives were in office and becoming more cautious about expansion and less open to the egalitarian movements confirmed by the Labour government which preceded them.

But from 1973 onwards, uncertainty, not only about the ability of the economy to carry increased educational expenditure, but also about the fruits of educational development began to be voiced from outside the system. The progressive mode in primary and secondary schools, the results of having so many students in full-time education, the ability of the educational system to benefit the economy and, for that matter, to expound and reinforce the minimum decencies of social life, were all placed in doubt.

MEETING INCREASED EXPECTATIONS, 1944–64

The first of our periods seems, in retrospect, a long era of contented growth and opportunity, although we can see more clearly now how meeting expectations never fails to create a corresponding disappointment. It is possible to view the years between 1944 and 1964 in terms of three interwoven themes: the rise of expectations as to how the Opportunity State will offer widened educational chances as part of the good life; the related expansion of the economy and changing distribution of its products; and demographic pressures and fluctuations. Against these backgrounds we can then look at the particular provisions made for education.

In 1950, the Ministry of Education celebrated its fifty years of life by publishing an historical account of its development. The minister, George Tomlinson, and the permanent secretary, Sir John Maud, who signed the report, declared the ministry's work to have been dictated by the following aims:

> To build a single, but not a uniform, system out of many diverse elements; to widen educational opportunity and at the same time to raise standards; to knit the educational system more closely into the life of an increasingly democratic and industrialised community; these are among the main ideas which, despite two major wars, have moved legislators and administrators alike.

In 1945, hardly a single public figure opposed the expansion and improvement of the education service. They could not have forecast how expansion would bring with it massive doubts and uncertainties about what constituted improvement. The President of the Board of Education in the wartime Coalition Government, R. A. Butler, has recounted in *The Art of the Possible* how he was able to get on with the drafting and the passing of the Education Act, 1944, with hardly a flicker of interest from Churchill and his Cabinet colleagues. It had been a long time since the Poet Laureate, John Masefield, could write, 'Better a humble, servile nation, than one that lives above its station'. Schools would help people to become more skilful and therefore more productive. Education would enable them not only to contribute

28

towards the economy but also towards a more civilised life for them and for their fellows. The fruitful use of leisure, the enhancement of relations between people, the increased wealth, freedom and elegance of lifestyle, all of these would come from education. These were views held equally by, say, a Labour minister such as George Tomlinson who was in power from 1948 to 1951 or a Conservative such as David Eccles who was in office, at intervals, between 1956 and 1962. They both assumed, perhaps not explicitly in the case of Tomlinson, that social objectives could be met through satisfying individual objectives of education. All seemed to agree on the value of education. Only for a remarkably short period, in the early 1950s, were there rate payers' protests about the cost of the 'glass palaces' being built by education authorities.

The contents of the Act are now, thirty-three years later, revealing in what they show of the best opinions then of educational progress. That all children should have eleven years of compulsory full-time education had already been argued in such pre-war official reports as those of the Hadow and Spens Committees. That all should receive secondary education had also been argued. Before the 1944 Act, secondary education had meant selective education for the minority. None seemed to object to the way that the very phrase should now be demoted or democratised (according to one's point of view) so as to include children of all abilities. Previously, children were sorted out into the majority who completed elementary education at fourteen, and a minority (13 per cent in 1938) who were given scholarships, or who paid fees, to complete a secondary school course at sixteen years, of whom an even smaller minority went on to the sixth form and higher education.

From 1945, however, secondary education was to be provided through a 'tripartite' system which allocated about 75 per cent of pupils to secondary modern schools and the rest either to grammar or to technical schools. It was a step forward in establishing a more egalitarian but selective educational system. Fee paying in local authority schools was made illegal. The school leaving age was to be raised in stages, from fourteen to sixteen years.

All schools were to enjoy 'parity of esteem'. Great efforts were made to ensure that the tripartite system provided everything everybody might need. During the David Eccles, Geoffrey Lloyd and Edward Boyle administrations, large sums of money were poured into the secondary modern schools which for a long time took the cream of the Ministry of Education building programmes. Many of them developed GCE O-level courses, and thus implicitly raised the question of whether there could be all that much difference between many of the pupils in secondary modern schools and those in grammar schools. All-age schools, catering for children from five to fifteen, were finally abolished. Teachers' salaries were restructured so as to reduce the premium enjoyed by the good honours graduate teacher who characteristically was to be found in grammar schools.

To many the system seemed democratic and fair. Ellen Wilkinson and George Tomlinson, the Ministers of Education in the first post-war government, defended the tripartite system. They did not doubt that children could be selected accurately for different courses from the age of eleven. It was not until the 1959 Party Conference that the Labour Party for the first time fully endorsed the principle of comprehensive education for all, though a 1951 manifesto had stated it as policy. From the time of the 1944 Act the Labour Party had been ambivalent about comprehensive education (see M. Parkinson's *The Labour Party and the Organization of Secondary Education 1918–1965*). Some teachers had opposed selection, as did a minority of local Labour parties, including those such as Middlesex and London County Council which in vain had tried to get first Labour and then Conservative ministers to approve the amalgamation of grammar and modern schools into comprehensive schools. Neither administration had been prepared to approve comprehensive schools except where an increased demand for school places made it possible without the abolition of an existing grammar school.

When the Labour Party came into power in 1945, the small group of advocates for comprehensive education in the National Association of Labour Teachers and elsewhere found little support from the top leadership. Although the Labour Government would always favour educational expenditure, such major figures as Aneurin Bevan or Emmanuel Shinwell, capable of delighting the more radical constituencies in the Labour Party, rarely concerned themselves with education.

For a long time, the leading theme of Labour Party policy was meritocratic: expand the number attending school, build more schools, improve the whole educational system, provide free secondary education for all, and give access to grammar and higher education for all able young people. It was not yet understood that simply to make opportunities open to all would mean that the stronger rather than the weaker members of the community would benefit most by getting access without fees to selective education. As grammar schools ceased to charge fees, the proportion of middle-class entrants increased. The social composition of the groups entering universities also remained biased towards those from the higher socio-economic classes. It was much later that sociologists and psychologists identified the fact that not only does social background determine educational achievement but that the concept of equality and remedies for inequality are ambiguous. It was Anthony Crosland who, in attacking the place of the public schools, in *The Conservative Enemy* (1962), first wrote of the weak and of the strong concepts of equality (also called the 'soft' and the 'hard' concepts). The strong concept assumes that it is necessary to compensate for poor backgrounds whereas the weak assumes that all can compete equally and that it is necessary simply to equalise competitive chances for social justice to be achieved.

But access to all of these opportunities depended on the

child, and his parents' ability to get him on to the right ladder at the age of eleven. Only about 2 per cent of children could transfer between different types of secondary education once allocated to a particular school. Studies made later from the 1950s showed that perhaps 15 per cent of pupils, as later assessed on entry to military service in Britain, and as shown in studies conducted in Stockholm by Torsten Husen, were allocated to the 'wrong' schools. The 'alternative ladder' corrected these faults to only a limited extent: only 23 per cent of those gaining Higher National Certificates or Diplomas in the 1950s did not come from selective schools.

Outside the schools, the psychologists, having first created educational testing and declared it fair and efficient, then discovered its inefficiencies; whilst sociologists, as early as the 1940s, but more strongly in the 1950s and 1960s, showed that making grammar school places open without charge to all able children caused the proportion of middle-class children taking places to rise rather than fall. As many studies have shown, all Welfare State services are understood and enjoyed most by those who have smallest need of them. The role played by the social science intelligentsia in causing change in this period was indeed striking.

But many parents did not oppose grammar school education because they wanted it for their own children. They would have applauded Harold Wilson's astonishing statement just before the 1964 election in favour of grammar schools for all, a precept adopted only by a few Welsh local authorities. To the parents of children growing up in the late 1940s and 1950s, the vistas of opportunity had opened up. Working-class boys and some girls could get to Oxbridge on full grants. Thus an undergraduate reaching Cambridge in 1950 was eligible for £288 plus full tuition fees, an amount sufficient to keep him adequately if he was prepared to find perhaps another £40 or £50 by vacation work which was not difficult in a Cambridge academic year of twenty-four weeks. He would then have what seemed to be an open sesame to

3

jobs in education, industry or, if able enough, in the administrative civil service or in academic work. If not to university, an adolescent could hope to get up the 'alternative ladder' in further education.

The Conservatives, following their belief in increased opportunity, expanded the universities and set in motion an even larger expansion which was to be achieved mainly during the Labour administration of 1964–70. They also created a further education system which would make it possible for those who had left school at fourteen, fifteen or sixteen to scale the heights of a technical education. They built up the technical colleges and the colleges of advanced technology.

The 1944 Act also said that all pupils were to have compulsory education for one day a week until the age of eighteen in county colleges, a provision never enacted. And, quite alone throughout the world, Brit.sh youngsters who stayed at school and went on to university or further education would be eligible for local authority or ministry awards if their courses were of a degree level. This became mandatory on local authorities in 1956.

Within the Eccles era (1956–62, with some gaps) pressure built up with his active encouragement for the vast expansion of higher education. In 1963 this was made respectable by the Robbins Report. The Robbins Committee, led by an eminent and entirely untrendy economist, endorsed the notion, based on social science research, that there was no fixed reservoir of talent, and that therefore there would be enough able youngsters to fill a greatly expanded system. So, universities were expanded or newly created and the number rose from twenty-four to forty-four in the 1960s. Thirty polytechnics were designated which, with the enlarged colleges of education, now offering a three-year rather than a two-year course, would offer degree level courses for virtually all who came forward with the minimum qualifications.

There were increased demands for a teaching force, and

for a training system which had to be massively expanded to service it. Elementary and rural all-age schools were abolished in 1945 and 1956 respectively. At one time as many as two new schools a day were being built and one a fortnight opened in Lancashire county alone. Technical colleges were filled virtually on the day that they opened. Through them the unqualified could become craftsmen or technicians, or go on to degree courses.

The pressure on university places in the late 1950s and early 1960s became intense as more pupils stayed at school, more gained the entry qualifications, more parents had money in their pockets so as to be able to tolerate or encourage their children to stay at school beyond the compulsory retention age, and as student grants became universal. A wider range of jobs required more advanced qualifications, and the professions and sub-professions of an increasingly sophisticated industrial society expanded in range and in numbers and thus stoked up demand for courses.

David Eccles was perhaps the minister who best typified the optimism and opportunism of the time. He succeeded a dreary and disliked minister who was brought only late into the Cabinet, who never fought for and never received an adequate educational budget. For example, Eccles bumped up the further education building programme from £5 million to £30 million in one year. And this at a time when, for example, no new hospital building was contemplated by the Ministry of Health. By the end of the 1950s he could sum up the optimism about economic growth and about social mobility which underpinned his policy of improving rural education and abolishing all-age schools by pouring more resources into education: he predicted that poverty would be abolished in the next decade. At the end of 1960, a Conservative junior minister could say, in a speech to the House of Commons: 'We are now having to reinforce the success of the earlier education drive which began some years ago and is now producing as its fruits an intensified demand for more and better education everywhere in the country'. Many present expenditures express past commitments and the momentum of expansion that was begun much earlier. They were so confident then.

Edward Boyle built up the system that Eccles did so much to create. Boyle brought Conservative democracy and liberalism to the fore. He empathised with the desires of all people to improve their range of choice and their freedom of lifestyle. He had little patience with doctrinaire elitism, with 'the voices hailing from All Souls saying that Robbins was a great mistake'. He was the minister who secured Cabinet approval for the expansion of higher education in 1963. He supported the progressive mode of primary education. These two Conservative ministers between them thus gave dynamic and style to the educational advances associated with opportunity.

DEMOGRAPHY AND THE TEACHERS AS STAKE-HOLDERS

In 1945 the schools and colleges waited quiescently for an upturn in their clientele. The end of the war in Europe brought with it a large wave of demands for places in higher education, in the universities, further education and colleges of education. Demand for the latter grew particularly fast because the same generation began to produce children, the first cohorts of whom hit the primary schools in the early 1950s. From then on the education system was inevitably caught in a wobbling cycle of population waves and troughs. The primary schools, then the secondary, and then the further and higher education system experienced first large expansions of numbers and then temporary declines. The figures of live births received from the Registrar General became important policy parameters for DES officials and ministers. But the recurrent theme over time, thus far, has been that of expansion as the Table on page 26 showed.

Post-war Britain was dominated by a belief in the better distribution of goods and other benefits, and by a belief in economic expansion. These two beliefs justified the expansion of the education and other public services. It has only been in the most recent years that the expansionist optimism of the 1950s and 1960s has come into doubt as 'steady state' doctrines have come into force. The expansion of the 1960s had effects which only now are beginning to be seen. The schools, universities and colleges became larger, and with them the promotion prospects and career pyramids of those *then working* in them. Expectations thus banked up in the 1960s. But promotion is good for the generation being promoted and bad for those who come just behind. The expansion of higher education was far more dramatic than even that of the schools, as the figures in Table 1 show. But it meant that whilst many academics became professors in the universities in the late 1960s and early 1970s, whilst still in their thirties, people of equivalent ability who were five years younger and who are working in a system that is likely to stay still rather than expand, will occupy the opportunity trough which always follows an opportunity wave. The same is beginning to be true of the schools. The birth rate turned down again in 1962. The school population will soon reach a peak and then go down until in the mid-1980s there will be perhaps one-and-a-half million fewer children in the schools than now. In the late 1970s there will be fewer pupils and fewer schools, for schools have begun to be combined.

So the somewhat joyous expansion of the 1960s must be seen in the perspective of what is now following. The demography and expansionism of the 1960s have undoubtedly affected educational politics in the 1970s. If the economy had continued to expand, falling or steady pupil and student populations would not affect teacher opportunities because the economy could afford better education through improved teacher ratios. But the declining demand for education coincided with, and was probably related to, a decline in the economy. From being required to increase its number of places from 24,000 in 1958 to 75,000 within a decade, the teacher training system is now having to reduce to 45,000 places. The teaching profession can no longer be secure in the knowledge that all comers will be appointed and all appointees will stand a good chance of senior posts if they stay the course because new schools, new colleges, new training and advisory posts, are opening up all around them. As a result, militant teacher politics have been given a sharper edge, and while teachers are certainly better protected than many industrial workers, they are now threatened by redundancy and reduced opportunities.

When opportunities were poor in the 1930s teachers suffered but in one respect their pupils did not. The depression meant that the schools could pick and choose among those whom they wished to employ and, as was true of all of the public services in the depressed years before the war, able people were recruited for front line jobs. It is true again that schools can choose, but security of tenure and the increasing power of the teachers' associations in protecting established positions in the teaching force make it less certain that the benefits of a free market in labour will be felt by the schools.

These difficulties were not, however, perceived in the 1960s. The connection between economic growth and educational advance seemed firmly secured. *The National Plan* (1965) declared:

education is both an important social service and an investment for the future. It helps to satisfy the needs of the economy for skilled manpower of all kinds, the needs of any civilised society for educated citizens who have been unable to develop to the utmost their individual abilities, and the demands by individuals for education as a means both to improve economic prospects and to a richer and more constructive life.

And it went on to state explicitly that teacher recruitment policies are necessary to prepare for a continued rise in the school population in the 1970s.

Thus the period 1945 to 1965 was one of expansion of the

economy and of education and of the expectations of both. The thrust forward in education was the result of demographic expansion and of economic expectation, and educational politics were largely consensual in their belief in expectation. The ministers of the period, particularly David Eccles and Edward Boyle, put their considerable gifts and commitment behind these policies. But both the motives and the economic viability of yet more expansion were soon to be thrown into doubt.

Chapter 3 The Onset of Doubt, 1964–77

The system was, then, expanded and the numbers committed to its future expansion grew with it. We have already seen, however, that doubts about equal opportunity began to grow as the defects of a 'fair' selection system began to be perceived. Opportunities were there more than ever before, but the gap between opportunity and its satisfaction, between opportunity and equality, became more evident.

The dissatisfactions that expansion brought with it can, again, be aligned with the division between individual and social objectives. Individual objectives were not achieved and the political effects have been to increase dissatisfaction with the public system both among middle-class parents who look for more from it and among the more radical groups who too look for both personal autonomy and freedom in the educational process and changes in its institutional formats. The social objectives were only partly achieved because increased opportunity did not heal the division between classes and did not bring full equality of life chances in its wake, even though redistribution and public investment had been massive.

The consequences of the growth of opportunity on educational politics were dramatic and multiple. It increased the numbers and range of stake-holders in the educational system. It meant that many more families developed expectations of what education could do. But increased expectations are never satisfied. Those who got admission to the courses and the qualifications they wanted then discovered that education may give opportunities but does not of itself change individual destinies or society. The exploitation of opportunity takes the individual on to yet further problems of how well motivated he is and what his ultimate purposes are; and these are answerable by the individual and not by a public system. The more we get the more we want, while those who do not share in the new opportunities become even more dissatisfied than they would have been if the opportunities had not been nearer their own grasp. And this was so even before graduate unemployment became a nightmarish reality.

This characteristic is known in sociology and social policy writing as the problem of relative deprivation. We feel deprived if our needs are not met. But our perception of what we need is based on moving and relative expectations created by our social groupings and by the general norms and expectations of our times. (See W. G. Runciman's *Relative Deprivation and Social Justice*, 1972; and *The Poor and the Poorest* by B. Abel-Smith and P. Townsend, 1965.) Thus it has been argued that had the vast majority of pupils gone to secondary modern schools whilst only a tiny proportion, say 2 or 3 per cent as against 20 to 25 per cent, went to a grammar school, secondary moderns would have been acceptable to the mass of the people. It is the difference between envying a neighbour his Rolls Royce and his house in the South of France and coveting his washing machine. The washing machine is now within most of our grasps; we resent its absence more than that of a villa in Cannes.

The aggrieved stake-holders were not only those who wanted grammar school education for their children and who could not get it. There were also those who went on to higher education and either found that they did not get to the place of their choice or that taking an undergraduate course was no guarantee of a good job or even of three years' spirited happiness. No young and eloquent Bertrand Russell or Maynard Keynes walks into undergraduates' rooms at X polytechnic or Y technological university. Not everybody visits Brideshead.

Although educational investment thus rose sharply, social harmony was never more in doubt than at the end of the period of expansion when the Heath government collapsed in 1974 after debilitating strikes that helped carry Britain into an inflation only comparable with Italy (where educational opportunities are pitiful) or the fascist regimes of South America. So far from education creating happiness, in its expanded form it seemed to accompany deep student dissatisfaction or apathy, a lack of certainty of destiny and, to some, an erosion of concepts of learning. Certainly the critics were too pessimistic and attributed difficulties to the wrong causes. Other countries where education remained repressive and instrumental had even more powerful student riots. Other countries where educational opportunity had widened and the formats became more free had strong economies. But by the end of 1977 only the daring or the self-interested were able to call for more educational growth as a certain way to economic and social salvation.

Expansion, then, driven by demography and by the assumption that economics and education went together, was one dynamic. Only later did other and sharper themes begin to be dominant. The hard concept of equality became legitimised in bi-partisan groups such as the Plowden Committee. The intellectuals, having discovered that the Welfare State had not enabled all to participate in the country's expanded wealth, that the poverty line moved forward with its remedies, because expectations advanced at the same time, went on to note that the barriers between people and their rights were 'attitudinal'. It is no use making better educational provision if people are not taught how to receive benefits.

The education profession and the politicians representing the system led the demand for growth. Such a minister as David Eccles or an educational leader as William Alexander, for thirty years the secretary of the Association of Education Committees, were not coy at stating their needs. There were demands, too, from industry and commerce for more highly educated people, although at this distance it is not clear whether industry really thought through why it wanted them. Neither in its working ways nor in its structure has industry created a place and an effective demand for technologists and it has not given the status which in its turn would stoke up demand for technological education in the schools and colleges. It may well have merely extrapolated its undoubtedly real demands for technicians and craftsmen into an assumption that even more highly educated people would be even more useful.

The growth of opportunities in higher education was accompanied by far more complex changes in the secondary schools. There is no change in fashion or of lifestyle that they have not experienced. They have borne the main burdens and benefits of the democratisation of education. It is they who took the first unwilling cohorts of those compelled to stay at school beyond the age of fourteen and then of fifteen years.

It was they who also took the brunt of the vast increase of voluntary staying-on which so swelled the exam-taking figures and the sixth forms and thus gave the lift-off to higher education expansion. It was they who first experienced the growing disenchantment with educational systems that purported to offer equality through separate but equal systems. It was they who suffered the amateurism of planners who in the critical post-war period assumed that schools must be inhumanly large to offer a full range of courses, the type of assumption that also committed Britain's Welfare State to mammoth hospitals and blocks of flats.

In the schools the political movements of the time, too, were faithfully reflected. The decline in formal authority, challenges to the hierarchy of head and administrator, militancy that takes a highly visible minority of teachers out of school in protest at virtually any of the grievances and concerns that might affect political man, all of these changes built up in the schools from the early 1960s. Yet with all this there are the conspicuous merits of our age. There is a growing concern for the child, as evinced by the growth of the pastoral or caring systems in the schools, by an adaptation of curriculum to individual needs and away from the artificial rigours of academicism, a concern for the less able child that reflects the other less raucous, more humanistic and constructive side of egalitarian radicalism. On these issues the traditional progressivism of British education seems to join hands with those Marxists who seek to reduce alienation and anomie.

Both those in favour of expansion for the sake of opportunity and those in favour of education because it was an equaliser had thought education could improve society. This was still firmly assumed in the National Plan of 1965 and in the Plowden Report on Primary Education of 1967. But in the late 1960s dissatisfaction became obvious, consensus was less certain, and optimism more precarious. The first sustained doubts about the Plowden Report's progressivism appeared in 1968 (see *Perspectives on Plowden*, ed. Richard Peters). Universal manifestations of student dissent occurred in the same year. By 1968, too, whilst the education system continued to expand, the indicative planning underlying expansion became less credible.

Moreover, increased educational access seemed to make the many less rather than more happy; it being true, of course, that those now enjoying opportunities from which their parents were excluded know nothing of the relative joys of inclusion over the frustrations of exclusion. The economists, in an uncharacteristic fall from certainty, could no longer be sure of any demonstrable relationship between educational investment and economic growth, or even stability. The belief that education equalised opportunity became more tentative as the concepts of equality themselves became more confused and more open to debate. Studies appeared which showed that educational investment did not equalise educational opportunities and that even when it did, it did nothing to enhance social mobility. (See, for example, R. Boudon's *Education, Opportunity and Social Inequality*.)

And education as the great changer of men came under attack from **many** disparate quarters. There were those in the universities and polytechnics who demonstrated how knowledge was an artefact, the generation of which could be impugned as merely creating defence for the views, concepts and intellectual formats of restrictive and privileged minorities.

The beauty and efficiency of progressive primary education, so long extolled by ministers and by scores of evangelising American books and savants, came under attack as uncertainty about both purposes and standards grew. Provocatively named Black Papers, written by a group of academics, educationalists, writers and politicians focused these attacks and sold in very large numbers of copies. The institutions which conveyed education, and particularly the universities, came under radical attack at the same time as their standards were being castigated from the right. They were accused of perpetuating the division of labour and the separation of roles that they, as establishments with specialist tasks, reinforced. Headmasters and local authority administrators were challenged by radical teachers and dissatisfied parents. Vice-chancellors were reduced from the dignity of independent notables to that of managers of systems subject to attack from the radical student extreme left and to disdain from Whitehall and Westminster. Dismissal of teachers, expulsions or restraint of radical students became the subjects of court cases for the first time.

So in the last decade of our period many of the arguments about educational policies were concerned with whether mass institutions could respond well to what individuals needed and what society demanded. Current widespread scepticism about whether the political system and the Welfare State can interpret people's wants is an important ingredient of what follows. Whether disappointed or not, there were indeed large changes in expectations of and assumptions about education since 1945.

PRESENT UNCERTAINTIES

Increased opportunity, therefore, seemed the objective until it was demonstrated that it neither equalised chances nor satisfied those who found that participating in the better opportunities did not give them what they had hoped from schooling. These dissatisfactions in the latter part of our period were accompanied by changes in education which derived from and contributed to changes in the wider society. There were challenges to the authority of knowledge and to the institutions that conveyed it. There were increased militancy and unionisation in the teaching profession and increased demands for participation of conflicting groups which looked away from the traditional, ballot box methods of democracy as being ineffective and ultimately undemocratic. These movements produced pressures on the authority system to account for itself at the same time as it was asked to be participative.

All of these movements affected politics and politicians. The consensus period was essentially one when Conservative ministers such as David Eccles and Edward Boyle inherited the new conservatism forged in the Conservative Research Centre by Ian McLeod under the aegis of liberal Conservatives such as R. A. Butler. During the Macmillan period in British politics, Conservatives were prepared to regard an improvement of public services as part of the rewards that an opportunity state could offer to its consumers. At that time, the Labour Party, which has always wasted its time in Opposition, hardly kept up with the work of the intelligentsia which was beginning to express doubts about the distributive ability of policies that merely equalised opportunity. They, therefore, did not challenge the consensus policies of Eccles and Boyle but somewhat lamely supported expansion and a gradualist move towards comprehensive education. Only Anthony Crosland of the Labour leaders explicitly expounded the weakness of the soft concept of equality, and he later on did not accept that there had been a true consensus in education.

From the return of the Labour Government in 1964, consensus in many fields of politics was broken. The relatively tolerant attitude in Opposition of Edward Boyle and William van Straubenzee, or of Timothy Raison, towards the development of comprehensive schools gave way to far more resistant attitudes as exemplified in Margaret Thatcher's 1970 announcement, within three days of becoming Secretary of State, that she would reverse Labour policy requiring local authorities to advance towards complete comprehensive education. On higher education, it is true, the views as to main policies are virtually indistinguishable as between the two parties. Both support the binary system of higher education which divides institutions providing advanced courses into universities and into the public sector led principally by the polytechnics. Both were prepared to support modest expansion until 1972, the year in which Margaret Thatcher's White Paper indicated deceleration rather than cut-back. Both seem now prepared to let higher education continue on far less favourable economic terms and on 'steady state' assumptions rather than on the assumption that the demand for higher education will continue to grow. In all, however, there is pessimism and uncertainty about what good education does, and from being the favoured child of the Welfare State until the late 1960s it is now having to show what it does, and at what cost.

Changes in opportunity and in the perception of those who benefited from it was, then, one important dynamic. The reader might ask, however, how these major changes relate to politics. At one level, it is certain, the relationship is remarkably weak. We will see in Chapter 9 how the political parties reacted to, rather than initiated many of the changes in the major policies. The soft concept of equality was bi-partisan in its appeal. It was only when others had fashioned for them the hard concept of equality in terms of actual policies for comprehensive education or educational priority areas that the Labour Party espoused it as a principle. They did it haltingly but in the end with conviction and strength and, as I write, a majority of secondary school pupils, by a slender margin, it is true, attend comprehensive schools. The school system, however, is exceedingly strong in its ability to generate and sustain its own policies. The continuities are far stronger than are the changes.

Yet what has been described here, and what will emerge in more detail in the succeeding chapters, is how the institutional framework of the schools—local authorities, the central ministry, the teachers—is under challenge. The demands for greater participation, for deschooling, for debureaucratisation, and the attacks on established learning systems and received wisdom, are all evidence of strong forces bursting through an institutional framework which for a long while has been thought to be adequate to meet the needs of the mass of the people. It is a reflection on the quality of British political life that the necessary changes are not initiated decisively by the democratically appointed political leadership, but so often start at the fringe.

From 1964 to 1970 consensus had been broken in terms of the social objectives of education. There was no disagreement as yet about the relationship between economic growth and educational investment. The power of education to act as a sufficiently redistributive force, and the ability of the formal policy-making system to allow dissenting views to have a voice, began to come into doubt. The period from 1970 to 1974 was one in which the egalitarian movements of the previous six years were brought to a halt and expansionism severely tested by the economic crises that eventually helped to bring the Heath government to electoral defeat. Our present period, from 1974 to 1977, is one in which several themes come together. Economic expansion has ceased and with it the expansion of the education service.

The institutional fabric of education has been reiteratively challenged and although the more potent radical challenges have been refuted, public authorities are now far less confident of their right to make decisions on behalf of the whole society. The confident planning assumptions of the 1960s have now given way to the range of uncertainties.

PART TWO

Current Conflicts

INTRODUCTION TO PART TWO

As assumptions and expectations widened, so did the ambiguities inherent in both the Opportunity State and the Welfare State, and in this section the general movements will be illustrated through discussion of particular issues. From consensus between politicians and the school system itself, education became a cockpit of many of the political issues that have emerged in Britain since the war. Who will get what, who will have the power to decide, how public systems may be influenced by outside pressures; all of these issues became sharp and tensile within the British educational system.

As we have seen, education is a major citizen right, an individual asset as well as a social good. It touches on so many motives at once: individual ambition, social altruism, hope for a better society, political power and, perhaps most cogent of all, the hopes and fears of individual citizens for their children. Most people do not identify all of these motives lucidly. For most people, education is concerned with what their children whom they are compelled to hand over to the schools for a minimum of eleven years of their lives, do and will get out of it. But struggles about which individuals will get what convert themselves into the political issues of who will control the curriculum; shall it be teachers, parents, students or elected authorities? Thus the claims of teachers for professional power raise the issue of their accountability to the society and to their clientele. That accountability, in its turn, raises the question of whether the schools shall be managed by elected local authorities or whether councillors must share their power with parents and teachers. The teachers' claims to be treated as largely independent professionals concerned with clients' needs must be set against their own demands of the right to act as syndicalists, as a group concerned not only with salaries and working conditions but also with autonomy in running the schools. In higher education, the struggles are about who will control the curriculum and for what purposes, and who will govern the institutions in which curriculum is made, developed and related to changing categories of knowledge.

In the end, and whatever the ruling system, we might suspect that children will be taught in ways decided by teachers. The full-time professionals within institutions which they largely run get their way on most things. But what the professionals do is affected, if not determined, by outside pressures and many of the questions that have most recently taken the school system by storm centre on questions of who will decide what in terms of the curriculum. That issue leads on to the apparently larger issues of structure—whether there will be comprehensive or selective schools—and the changes in the representative system as embodied in the governing bodies.

These general issues flow into two particular issues, touched on in Chapters 8 and 9: the move towards greater equality in education and changes in higher education.

Chapter 4 The Struggle over Curriculum and Standards

HOW CHILDREN SHOULD BE EDUCATED

Debates about the curriculum and the way in which it is devised and administered are central to arguments about educational politics.

The English and Welsh schools have acquired a double reputation. One strand of the British tradition is liberalism in the modes of encounter between pupil and teacher and this has been characteristic particularly of the primary schools. But British education also has, or used to have, a high reputation for its academic quality, for the way in which its universities and academics, and the grammar and public schools that fed them, produced good scientists, writers, philosophers and administrators, and an impeccable judiciary. The belief in these two excellences, it is true, tended to ignore the education provided for the mass of children who left school at twelve, thirteen, fourteen or fifteen, these leaving ages being raised at long intervals since the turn of the century. Concern with the majority, has, in fact, added a third theme, that of social equality, which we deal with later.

In the period of reasonably comfortable consensus in British education, between 1945 and the early 1960s, the traditions did not seem seriously in conflict although primary teachers were always uneasy about what happened to their charges once they entered into the compartmentalised rigours of secondary modern and secondary grammar schools. Perhaps consensus, the fact that that peace could prevail between two apparently inconsistent traditions, depended on the way in which primary education did not really 'need' to be compatible with secondary education. It was possible, it might have been implied, for the younger children to be treated liberally and to follow their own interests on the understanding that they would soon buckle down to 'real' work once they transferred, at eleven, to grammar schools. So many middle-class parents were prepared to send their children to maintained primary schools where the atmosphere seemed good and the teachers nice, even if they were not convinced that skills were being strongly enough inculcated. Work would really begin in the fee-charging independent schools at a later stage. The progressivism of the primary school need hardly to defend itself as long as the able were chosen at eleven for selective schools although some parents might fear that penalties might accrue to the children who could not perform certain sets of tricks for the 11 + examinations if primary education were too progressive.

In this sort of argument, the problems of the less able in the primary and secondary modern schools were occluded as being less important. For a long while, the secondary moderns seemed to be so massive an improvement on the previous senior elementary schools and so much still settling down that the divisiveness they embodied did not seem politically interesting. One of the few debates in the House of Commons in the 1950s on secondary modern schools took place at 6 am after an all-night sitting on the Finance Bill. The Member raising the question of secondary modern schools was Horace King, later to be Speaker of the House of Commons, and he addressed an audience of one junior minister—as well as being listened to, somewhat unwillingly, by a government whip in compulsory attendance, a private secretary in the official box, and a plain-clothes policeman guarding the proceedings against potential disruption from the public gallery. Discontent with the secondary school divide was, for a long while, intra-institutional. Labour did not fight the 1964 election on the issue.

The differences between primary and secondary education have always been quite sharp. For some decades the primary schools developed progressive modes. By contrast, the secondary schools from the first point in their development at the beginning of the century were always concerned with training for particular skills as well as with infusions of the more general culture. It is true that reformers have tried to influence secondary schools with the best of the primary school traditions. These attempts were evident in such documents as the Newsom Report on the less able secondary school pupils (1963). The primary zone, at its best, used to embody what Julia Evetts calls the 'progressive concept', whilst the secondary selective system, again at its best, embodied the idealist concept of education. The one relied primarily on the interaction between pupil and teacher for the development of the child's potential. The other assumed that there were educational patterns, skills and categories of knowledge existing in an ideal world outside the school and able to be transmitted from one generation to another.

Part of the controversy about the introduction of comprehensive education is concerned with ending that gentle truce between the progressivism of the primary school and the rigourism that many hoped to see in the secondary school. Those who believe in comprehensives also believe in inducing the best aspects of the primary school into the secondary stage. For one thing, of course, primary schools are themselves comprehensives because there is no selection by ability into different schools.

There had been perhaps twenty or thirty years of triumphant progress by the primary schools in which it seemed that all that was good was happening through them. A powerful humanitarianism seemed to suffuse the best of the primary schools. To the visitor they seemed unbelievably good in their relationships between adults and children, able to elicit powerful interest on the part of the pupils, and yet still be highly productive in work that was both creative and skilful. Successive reading surveys since 1948 had shown that eleven-year-olds in 1964 were reaching the standards that children seventeen months older in 1948 had attained.

Against evidence such as this it was difficult for attacks on the primary schools to be sustained. The new mathematics in the primary schools seemed exciting and impressively difficult to those brought up in traditional maths.

The Plowden Report on Primary Education (1967) celebrated the achievements of the primary schools in several hundred pages. The committee shared the views of the liberal educational leadership that children do best when starting work from a basis of what interests them, when they learn from living experience rather than from the implantation of bits of learning or of skills. It was argued that basic skills of reading, writing and arithmetical computation follow as a secondary consequence of the child working on problems which interest him and that the mere mechanical exercise of skills is less important than learning to understand, to think for oneself, and to be able to work flexibly in a world where patterns of employment will constantly change. These assumptions had been promulgated as early as in the 1933 Hadow Report, also the product of a government-appointed committee. They were now confirmed in 1967 by a committee which included some of the ablest intellectuals, leading teachers and educationalists of the day.

It was not only British educational progressives who endorsed these developments. American educators, so appalled by the evident failure of their schools, repressive, instrumental and narrow as so many were, to induce either good academic standards or commitment to reasonable social behaviour, came to Britain and marvelled at and wrote prolifically about the British 'open' schools. And they were endorsed by such liberal Conservatives as Sir Edward Boyle and, in the event, more strongly by liberal middle-class opinion than by that of working-class parents who are more concerned, and with more reason, that their children should learn how to work in ways acceptable to the employment system.

But so far from the progressives having it all their own way, they began to lose ground towards the end of the 1960s in the primary schools. The critics got to work. An able group of academics at the London Institute of Education, led by Richard Peters, an educational philosopher, attacked the theory of progressivism in which was embodied the notion of child development. This argued that the child's innate ability and willingness to learn only awaited encouragement and nourishment by the provision of carefully constructed programmes through which the teacher could interact with him and stimulate him to move at his own pace forward into concepts and skills. Black Papers were written by a wider group of academics and teachers and literati and were deliberate and fairly crude attacks on both the principles and structure of the liberal mode. Without much confirmed evidence, the first two Black Papers associated progressive education with educational decline. Later on, an academic study by Neville Bennett (*Teaching Styles and Pupil Progress*, 1976) of one perhaps atypical area (Lancashire) seemed to demonstrate that progressive methods had no advantage in enhancing creativity and were less effective in teaching the traditional skills.

The same doubts but determination to advance in the progressive mode underpinned issues of curriculum and organisation in the comprehensive schools. During our period opinions changed. The earlier belief that children could be efficiently and fairly selected at the age of eleven gave way under the impress of psychological and sociological criticisms of the 11+ selection system. Secondary modern teachers began to be frustrated by the creaming off of the ablest children to grammar schools. Parents were at first content with the tripartite system but 60 per cent wanted grammar school places for their children. Increasingly, however, more believed that comprehensive education was fairest for all whilst still hoping that their own children would go to grammar school. Many teachers believed it was time to end selection at eleven and create a comprehensive system, but they had no clear support from the Labour Party until the late 1950s. As late as 1963, Harold Wilson assured the world that grammar schools would be abolished 'only over his dead body', one of the promises that he has not kept. As we have seen, the running had to be made mainly by a handful of local education authorities and by teachers devoted to the cause.

By the mid-1970s nearly a half of the children were in comprehensive schools and plans had been made to ensure that all but a small minority would be in comprehensive education by 1980. And once this position had been reached, all of the problems and ambiguities of comprehensive education became more apparent. The evidence on outcome was not so much mixed as incomplete, since the great majority of the British working population had been educated in schools other than comprehensives and the full process, which would involve the assimilation of all selective schools, had only just begun. Even so, there was some evidence that areas that had gone comprehensive increased the number of GCE O-level successes, perhaps as much because of wider access to courses as through any intrinsic merit in teaching in comprehensive schools. The move to comprehensive organisation meant that parents, teachers and administrators could no longer avoid conceptual and logistical difficulties of reconciling several different objectives at once. They needed to uphold standards of academic excellence and to ensure that the ablest were not short-changed. They needed to broaden curricula so that all children, including those with an academic bent, would be exposed to the teaching of broader social skills and attitudes. They needed to make sure that the backward and deprived received their share of teaching resources. The underlying doctrine was that of social cohesion. All of these had to be brought together into one school framework.

The reaction to the spread of comprehensive education was composed of many elements. There were those who had enjoyed selective education for the prestige and access to good careers that it brought them and their children. Teachers in grammar schools, too, could only be dismayed at the rebuke implied in the demolition of their forms of teaching. Many were ready to talk about a dilution of standards before the movement got underway. Comprehensive schools were assumed to be far too large to be humane, and many local authorities drastically revised the maximum figure that they deemed to be viable for educational purposes.

Such bodies as the Confederation of British Industries maintained that schools were not doing enough to encourage basic skill learning or motivation towards the applied sciences and arts that might help the manpower needs of industry and business. It is worth remarking, however, that there has never been an occasion upon which the employers' federations have not complained about the standards of the schools. In 1977, a knowledgeable Labour peer, Wilfrid Brown, in addressing a University Congregation, could by implication deplore the growth of comprehensive education by declaring the demise of the secondary technical schools to be one of the many contributions to our economic difficulties.

These pressures on the secondary and primary schools were not new. Some teachers have always had to resist the imposition on schools of narrow and instrumental purposes. The HMIs (inspectors of schools) who largely wrote the Newsom Report (1963) were at pains to discourage the secondary schools from teaching such rote skills as shorthand and typewriting. In further education, too, the proportion of general and liberal studies required for technical certificates and diploma courses increased greatly in the 1960s.

The new forms of secondary curriculum, however, aroused precisely the same doubts as did progressive primary education. It was one thing to reject false rigour, the learning by rote of dull if useful skills. It was quite another to produce the alternative that would embody pupil and teacher creativity, and at the same time ensure that pupils received adequate information and the build-up of skills, which in, for example, mathematics and the language arts seem to require continuing application. It is important to emphasise, however, that the progressive mode did not simply come from teachers who might be thought over-sympathetic to expressed feelings of their pupils rather than to some externally endorsed world of knowledge.

For example, there have been since the 1930s recurrent attempts to liberalise the system of secondary school examinations. In 1951, the old Higher School and School Certificate examinations gave way to the General Certificate of Education. Pupils no longer had to take five subjects at once, or to include English language and mathematics in their grouping of subjects. One O or A level can be taken at a time. The Certificate of Secondary Education introduced in the mid-1960s was an attempt to provide an examination for pupils not normally expected to take GCE examinations. But since its introduction in 1965 the Schools Council, with its majority of teacher members, has attempted to combine GCE and CSE into one examination. There are excellent educational reasons for this change. For one thing, teachers have to make exceedingly difficult choices as to which pupils will take one examination and which will take the other. For another thing, pupils have to be divided in their fourth and fifth year into two examination streams, a luxury which many schools cannot afford. At the same time, however, putting together examinations designed originally for different groups of pupils, even though Grade I passes are held to be the equivalent of an O-level pass, means some demotion of the status of the GCE examinations.

The doctrines underlying these changes are clear. Dividing children up is not only doctrinally unacceptable to many teachers but also extremely difficult as a tactical and logistical exercise. It means that too much is made of examinations which tend to dominate the curriculum if they are made too strong an influence. For these reasons, many teachers have wanted to see the total abolition of examinations. In this they have been joined by those who are not school teachers themselves. For example, a committee including two leading academic scholars of the English language (Randolph Quirk and Hugh Sykes-Davies), studying English-language examining in the mid-1960s declared that O-level examinations had an extremely bad effect on the level of learning of English in schools and they hoped that after a five-year trial period the examination would be abolished altogether.

Similar attempts to reconcile academic standards with freedom for the schools to find their own way can be found in many other areas of the curriculum. The separate, artificial study of history and geography, at least in the lower stages of secondary education, has given way to broader based integrated and environmental studies. Many scientists, too, would think that divisions between biology, physics and chemistry are artificial and that, in theory, the secondary schools are right to integrate science teaching. But integration of material, it can be argued, comes best from those who have first learnt the different components. It takes considerable academic knowledge as well as creative skill to put through the new forms of education which the leading teachers in comprehensive schools are trying to create. Moreover, they are trying to do these things at the same time as problems of discipline and authority are becoming sharper. A relaxation of set programmes is taking place in a period of some disorganisation and risk, and without clear understanding and support on the part of parents and those who eventually will employ the pupils.

At each turn, then, the secondary schools, in attempting to create new curriculum patterns, meet sensitivities on the part of their clientele. Because the schools do not accept the view that children can be rigidly separated according to ability, they are reluctant to 'stream' pupils according to ability. In practice, studies have shown how comprehensive schools tend to put children in ability streams although, increasingly, the first two years of secondary school life are integrated. But where pupils are separated out, it is an open question as to whether the principal duty of the school is to attend to the more able children, or to those who suffer educational disadvantage. Some of the remedial units in comprehensive schools are among the better developments in education of the last ten years. So are some of the sixth forms. But it is difficult to maintain both.

CENTRAL CONTROL AND DEVELOPMENT OF THE CURRICULUM

What part did the government, through the Department of Education and Science, play in these educational controversies? The DES is a powerful element in educational policy but its special relationship with the schools (see Chapter 9) does not make it easy for it to take a strong view on educational content even though it has 500 HMIs who potently influence what goes on in the schools.

Over time, the DES has always been unwilling to intervene on the content of education even if it has often been quite authoritative on issues of resources and of structure which affect the curriculum.

The political authorities concerned with education in, say, the late 1940s and early 1950s were certainly concerned to allow pluralism of content. There was no attempt to enforce a single curriculum. Yet the curriculum has not always been entirely free from government control. In 1902, the Board of Education ceased its system of 'payment by results' which related the amount of grant received by schools to the tested competence of their pupils. The control of the curriculum was then vested in the local school authorities. But the central government continued to exercise control through codes of practice for both primary and secondary schools. In the view of Maclure, one expert witness to the 1976 Select Committee sub-committee under the chairmanship of Janet Fookes, 'these codes prevented a whole lot of things from happening in secondary education and in advanced elementary education which ought to have been able to happen'. In

Maclure's view, however, change developed in the localities and after the war the codes were abandoned and freedom was conferred fully in the schools.

The authority which was once vested in the Department went to the local authorities, which by default passed it to the schools, and it has now got all the ivy encrusted tendencies of tradition, which has in fact only got a very few years behind it. But everybody believes that it has always been like that, and must go on being like that.

Curriculum has always been less controlled by the centre than in any other comparable society except perhaps contemporary Yugoslavia or Germany, where the provinces are strong whilst the central government is not. And from 1944 at least, successive ministers announced their belief in freedom for the schools to produce their own patterns of work because it was the best way to encourage creativity, a true response to pupils' needs, and good standards of committed work.

In 1965, the DES had attempted to enter what Sir David Eccles called 'the secret garden of the curriculum' by the creation of what he most unwisely labelled 'a commando type unit', the Curriculum Study Group (CSG). This group consisted of a few HMIs, administrators (including this author) and educational experts from the outside, and their task was to identify, analyse and publish accounts of curriculum development which might be of help and interest to the schools. Indeed most of their work, in the short period of time they were allowed to exist, consisted of preparing papers on methods of examining for the Secondary School Examinations Council. The ministry soon disbanded the CSG because of a wave of anxiety from the teacher associations who thought that it was an attempt to take on the control of educational content. Nothing could be further from the truth, for it was essentially an attempt to enable the ministry to inform others better as well as to clarify its own thinking about those aspects of the curriculum which should affect the larger policy decisions. There was internal struggle within the DES for some administrators wanted policy to be more closely affected by educational substance while others feared that no development would be safe for ever and the CSG should be located in a protected position away from the potential interference of reactionary ministers or permanent secretaries. 'We shan't be here forever', remarked one of the more progressive senior administrators. Eventually, the DES joined with the local authority associations and the teachers in creating the Schools Council for the Curriculum and Examinations. The Schools Council soon developed a large number of research and development projects. But it, again, suffered from precisely the same constitutional problems as underlie the struggles which we are describing in this chapter. For the majority of its members were from the teacher associations and it could not declare on the curriculum or on schools' examinations without being attacked as captive to established teacher opinion. It thus became an easy target for critics, including some whose contribution to the development of the maintained school system, once it had ceased to be chic to support it, had waned through the Wilson administrations. In 1977 Shirley Williams made decisive efforts to reduce teacher power in it and in this she might have been encouraged by the criticisms made by the 1976 sub-committee of the Expenditure Committee.

The attacks on the Schools Council were part of one important element of the attacks on educational consensus, namely on the power of the educational establishment. In 1976 as well, attitudes hardened towards the more liberal and progressive elements of education and these, too, were attacks on the educational establishment. The Prime Minister of the time, James Callaghan, himself a former member of Inland Revenue staff, where precision is all important, apparently on the advice of Bernard Donoghue

18

who provided him with views on short-term policy, had asked Fred Mulley, the Secretary of State for Education, to concern himself and the DES with the public anxiety about standards. Before Mulley transferred to become Ruler of the Queen's Navee, he ordered a confidential document known as the Yellow Book to be prepared. This document leaked in the press. It expressed doubts about the standards being achieved and though written by HMIs seemed to extend those doubts to the very methods that HMIs had prominently promoted for forty or so years.

This concern with standards tied up with the DES's revived interest in assessment of performance. An Assessment of Performance Unit had already begun to formulate models of different segments of the curriculum and ways in which samples of pupils throughout the country could provide policy-makers with information about the standards being reached. Terror strikes easily in the education establishment's breasts and this creation, together with some statements that seemed to lay the inefficiencies of the British economy at the feet of the schools, were thought to mean that the DES might take up a prescriptive role on standards. In fact, the Assessment of Performance Unit was not to concern itself with individual schools or individual authorities, but was to provide information on performance about the whole system and lead thinking on a common curriculum core.

Yet the DES was now moving towards slightly tougher attitudes on the curriculum. The introduction to the 1950 Annual Report of the Ministry of Education warned readers not to expect a substantial chapter on 'Educational method and curriculum of the schools':

The reason is that the Department has traditionally valued the life of institutions more highly than the system and has been zealous for the freedom of schools and teachers. In all matters, therefore, affecting the curriculum and methods of teaching, it has been content to offer guidance by means of 'Suggestions' and in the main to rely on Your Majesty's Inspectorate.

By 1976 the permanent secretary, in speaking to the Select Committee, thought the DES would like to see the ambiguities attaching to the Secretary of State's position in relation to the curriculum clarified. The Select Committee, indeed, said of the Assessment of Performance Unit that if their findings give cause for concern, 'we believe that the Secretary of State should not shirk his responsibilities for drawing attention to the facts and stimulating, or if necessary, strongly persuading appropriate action to be taken'. They added that they were extremely anxious that none of their proposals should be construed as a desire to see political interference in the work of the classroom.

As we write, the debate on standards is going on. There is no clear evidence either way as to what the changes have been, all the more since education means so many things at once that its measurement also means measuring several things at once. The primary school progressives and their comprehensive counterparts will complain, rightly, that it is not their task to teach children to act as second-class calculating machines or to learn to 'bark' at the print. There is in any case genuine uncertainty about what is happening. The Prime Minister's speech at Ruskin College in the autumn of 1976 obviously implied that standards had declined, or, at any rate, were not keeping up with current demands. Sir Alec Clegg, a leading progressive educational administrator whose primary schools in the West Riding were internationally renowned, retorted that if it were so 'that we can no longer teach children to read. . . . I am puzzled by the fact that Puffin Books increased their sales from 600,000 in 1961 to 6 million in 1975.' Yet the employer baffled by bad spelling and grammar in employees who spend eleven years of their life in learning the skills also have a point which is too easily ignored.

So far we have seen how the educational system was allowed to evolve its own consensus about progressivism in the primary schools and, for a far briefer time, to induce more liberal and comprehensive education in the secondary sector. These progressed almost as if they were professionally technical matters. But in the late 1960s challenges were beginning to be lodged. Middle-class opposition to comprehensive education at large was demonstrated in the Enfield case (see Chapter 7) and in the challenge to Fred Mulley by the Tameside Local Education Authority. But there was also strong evidence of some working-class alienation from comprehensive education as well. In some London areas parents tried to place their children in those comprehensive schools which had previously been grammar schools. Parents in North London, for example, kept their children away from school if they failed to get the school of their choice. Primary school progressivism was attacked through the successive Black Papers but came under the most exigent scrutiny after it had been advanced in its most extreme form at the William Tyndale Junior School.

The challenges so far discussed have been, it should be noted, in favour of strengthening of accepted assumptions. The critics do not seek radical change in education but a consolidation of knowledge, of skill learning and of the control of education for those purposes. Teachers are not so much under attack, as being propelled into a more strongly institutionalised stance in which their freedom to interact with pupils may be restricted but their authority to assert society's views of education's purposes might be made stronger.

Yet this theme, of reaction from progressivism, intermingled with the strongest attacks yet experienced from the left wing. It is to those that we now turn.

Chapter 5 Institutionalism Attacked and the Changing Power Structure

From the mid-1960s, politics and government underwent important changes of style and discourse of which education provided major examples.

In this chapter, and in Chapter 8 where we discuss higher education, we note two complementary but somewhat different themes. There were first drastic changes of attitude towards authority and demands that the specialist roles and status of teachers and the academic system should be reduced so as to diminish the effects of specialisation and the division of labour in society at large. The second set of changes were less radical but far more complex and concerned the issue to which we have already referred—who should control the schools?

The first of these themes was attack on authority and institutionalism. The second was compatible with a quite strong belief in institutionalism but demanded a realignment of power within the accepted structure. In place of local authority appointed governors, for example, the demand grew that governors and managers should be appointed from among the immediate clientele of the school and from the teachers and other employees who ran the schools.

Both of these conflicting sets of demands sought to reduce the classic ballot-box type of participation and substitute more direct intervention by particular groups in society. Whilst ballot-box democracy, inert and stodgy as it might have been, was concerned to take a synoptic and overall view of the needs of the community, the new demands were essentially atomistic or particular. They allowed different groups not so much to seek consensus as to represent directly their own particular viewpoint without any logical or moral requirement to state the needs of all. The defence of bureaucracy and of ballot-box democracy has always been that they can take a detached and impartial view of the needs of everybody. But their assumed weaknesses of bureau-cratisation and remoteness have been argued as justification for consumerist and syndicalist interventions in the democratic process.

Britain and its Welfare State have hitherto relied on strong arrangements for the creation and carrying out of policies. While we have never approached the formality of statement and structure of, say, France or Sweden or Germany, we have assumed that our officials are efficient, equitable and honest, that our public arrangements are the product of sane if unpretentious discussion and compromise, and that people should and will conform to them. Society has assumed that good can be achieved by publicly created systems whose roles, resources and functions incorporate the belief that they do good. This is the assumption summed up by the word institutionalism of which the schools have been a prime example.

Moreover, the DES, the local authorities, the educational administrators, the heads and teachers, have exercised authority and power which derived partly from the knowl-edge which the teachers imparted to pupils, and on which their professional status was based, and partly because they were all part of a system expected to control large numbers of young people during some of the more formative and turbulent years of their life. The DES expected to get away with persuasion on many policies. It did not expect its very ways of working to be held up to attack or criticism.

In the 1950s and 1960s there was a general change in atti-tudes towards authority. This was experienced in the general culture. There were savage attacks on Macmillan, in some ways the ablest and most dignified post-war premier, particularly associated with his gentlemanly acceptance of John Profumo's word that he had not slept with Christine Keeler. There was the growth of satire against political, business and academic institutions, on the radio, television and in the printed word. Informality and permissiveness grew. First names were used. Mixed housing for students became accepted, though certainly unacceptable in previous years.

In the schools the movement was not clearly set in one direction. Parental opinion favoured rigour and discipline, except for some middle-class liberal minorities who remained faithful to the progressivism of primary schools and hoped for a continuation of it in the new comprehensive system. Teacher opinion has certainly favoured the loosening of formal and traditional educational methods in relation to pupils. In relation to the larger system, teachers have been concerned with two interlocking uncertainties: are teachers full professionals whose dependence on hierarchy should be loosened? And, if so, how can they be denied a place in the government of the school even if that place must be reconciled with others who are also demanding a place?

The schools became the centre of conflicts between different groups who wished to control them. Schools are traditionally run by the heads who manage them, within broad discretion, on behalf of the local education authority, which is an elected county or metropolitan district council. The council shares some of its authority with the governing or managing bodies upon which, except in the case of voluntary aided schools, a majority of local authority nominees sit. In the past, the governing body which formally has control 'over the curriculum and conduct' of the school was a constitutional confection of no great importance. The head and local authority effectively determined the educational policy of the school. They thus demonstrated traditional or ballot-box democracy. The head was ultimately under the local authority's control and the local authority was supposed to ensure democratic input because it faced the electorate every four years. But the problem with that formula was that neither local authority officials nor the head faced the electorate and, indeed, if parents were asked, they might have been glad of the fact because they expected the schools to provide expertise and continuity rather than give in to democratic urges.

In the 1960s important change occurred, not in law, but in reality. In only a minority of areas, perhaps, but politically significant for all that, parental and other non-party voices began to make their views heard. The Confederation for the Advancement of State Education, created in the early 1960s, attempted to get parental voices heard in the schools and also to get parents involved in the work of the schools more directly. A bit later on, teachers became more militant and expected places on governing bodies.

The arguments now developed were complex and self-contradictory. A school must serve and reflect the strengths and needs of its immediate neighbourhood. So, directly appointed parents should serve on the governing bodies. This argument was cogently advanced by the National Association of Governors and Managers and accepted by, for example, the Inner London Education Authority (ILEA) and in 1977 the Taylor Committee on School Government. Secondly, and contradictorily, there were demands that the head and representatives of other teachers should be members of the governing body to secure better participation by those who worked in the school. The same demands began to be extended on behalf of non-teaching staff. Some schools, as well, included one or two pupils, but in attendance rather than membership, it being illegal to appoint members under eighteen. Thus participation has two faces: control by the clientele and control by the professional. Participation also argues for the appointive power of elected local authorities to be reduced and the Taylor Committee has recommended that governing bodies should consist of one quarter local authority, one quarter parents, one quarter teachers and one quarter other 'community' representatives. If this passes into law, it will go counter to the institutional tradition upheld by such a leading Labour politician as Herbert Morrison. He was determined that institutions should not be run by those who work in them or by their immediate clientele, but by the local authority that stands for election by the wider constituency. The dangers Morrison conceived were those of self-interest if employees help govern institutions where they earn their own livings, and parochialism by clients who might insist that a school be run in terms of their own narrow ideas rather than those of a wider society and a strong educational expertise. Against these claims it would be argued that local authority control of the school has meant that the party hacks and the bureaucrats run the schools between them.

A further complication asserted itself as local education authorities—the county and metropolitan district councils who run the schools—pushed forward with notions of managerial efficiency. Education participated in the tide wash of management theory which tends to subject the decisions made by professionals to the tests of priorities, costs and programming of the larger local authority system. At least two local authorities have attempted to introduce the system known as Programming, Planning and Budgeting (PPB). Corporate managers try to make education more accountable to the whole local authority and not just to the education committee, to the point where one director of education, in Avon, resigned because he said that he could no longer feel that he had control of the institutions for which he was held accountable; decision-making was diffused so seriously throughout different committees of the authority that the heads no longer knew where to turn for guidance or for decisions.

The corporate management doctrine is an important demonstration of how unreflecting adoption of a simple concept can cause more harm than good. Within local authorities there is certainly a crying need for a clearer attribution of functions as between education, social work, housing, planning, recreation and services such as police and health which are not administered by the local authority. Unfortunately, corporate management has been seen as a mode of rationalising resource control rather than as an attempt to clarify overall purposes and get orderly working together.

Attempts to bring teachers to heel in the interests of corporate management have, in fact, failed, although there have been no pitched battles. Teachers and the schools are strong institutions in their own right. It is not possible to programme their work or to be clear about their outcomes or to persuade them that either intellectual exercise is worth much of their time.

The new mechanistic management movement therefore fell short of meeting demands for accountability if by that is meant identifying expected outcomes and the exacting of penalties for failures to meet performance targets. Instead, and in the view of this author, fortunately, the issue has been whether teachers are entitled to state and insinuate their own values into the educational process and, by extension, into educational techniques, and if so, on what terms.

Here, too, different perspectives can be given. The most startling case was that of William Tyndale. In that school, methods were highly permissive and strongly ideological. It was alleged, for example, that pupils were taught to play Monopoly so that they could discover how the capitalist system worked. Accountability was in fact brought into the question by a group of managers who had been urged to it by the strong evidence that the school was declining in roll as alarmed parents removed their children from it. As a result, the local authority, its inspectorate and the managers were reprimanded in the report of an independent inquiry which asserted the duty of those elected or appointed to intervene when standards of work are poor. The teachers had virtually insisted on their professional right to teach how and what they please—a view never sustained, incidentally, by their unions.

COLLEGIAL AND HIERARCHICAL VIEWS

Teachers have thus had to face demands from within the local authorities for accountability and corporate management; and growing concern from outside for their performance to be assessed. But within the schools themselves new views are beginning to be expressed.

There is first the issue of what should be the relationship between professional control and the work of the governing bodies (known as managing bodies in primary schools). Governing bodies have many roles. They are mainly appointed by the local authority and are part of the accountable political system. They increasingly are expected to represent parents or clients of the system and they are also expected to represent teacher or employee views—as teacher governors and managers are appointed.

The governing body thus has more than one perspective upon which it has to work and more than one line of responsibility. It is doubtful whether it can at one and the same time respond to ballot-box democratic views, to the syndicalism of teacher representation and to consumerism.

The governing body also has to relate as a whole to the work of the teacher in the school. If teachers are the full-time professionals it follows that they are licensed to create curriculum and internal organisation but in so doing they are expected, implicitly, if not overtly, to respond to social expectations. If there is conflict, there is also reference to the local authority.

But within the schools, opinions divide on how they should be organised and, again, they respond to current movements in opinion within British society as a whole.

Schools are traditionally hierarchical. The official terminology implies this, for the head does not have colleagues but 'assistants'. Since the war the salaries structure has made for a far more elaborate hierarchy in which there might be more than one deputy head, as well as heads of houses, heads of faculties, heads of years, and the more traditionally used heads of departments in secondary schools at least.

Some teachers have maintained that schools should become collegial rather than hierarchical. There are, in fact, three possible perspectives on this. The first is that since the school must be coherent and unambiguous in the work that it does, there has to be a single accountability for the school focused on the head. Alternatively it is suggested that because a school is an amalgam of individual practitioners working with pupils in a creative and individual fashion, the school should be either collegial or collective. But a collegium is an institution which provides only minimum controls over its members and they include the distribution of collective resources and the setting of collective minimum standards. Collegia are only appropriate where coherence and collective decision-making are not at a premium. So those who do not like hierarchy but who believe that a school should be coherent in its work are attempting to create collectives. A collective is an institution in which not only minimum standards and resource-sharing are decided, but the total process is performed by virtue of collective authority and responds to collective decision-making.

In practice, our schools are still hierarchical. It would be impossible to find a school within the maintained system which is not. But hierarchies are changing and increasingly many decisions are delegated from the head to committees within the school which determine the creation of curriculum, the general arrangements for running the school and so on. These vary greatly in the authority given them and heads vary enormously in the style which they adopt. Some talk democracy and are highly authoritarian. Others do not bother at all with committee systems but gently and implicitly share a great deal of their authority with colleagues.

Because the school is an institution where the nerves are on the surface, where individual feelings directly affect working style and ability, where interaction between individuals of all ages is at a premium, the education system is indeed a central area at which the current demands for working democracy are most loudly heard. These demands are made not only for teachers but also for the non-teaching staff who are often 'gate keepers' through whom parents make inquiries or complaints. Caretakers, who are responsible for the physical integrity of buildings which are used for an increasing range of purposes, are felt to have a right to join the discussion about the purposes for which schools are used.

So far, the questions of institutionalism have been discussed in terms of the radical movements in higher education and the rejection of ballot-box democracy, by at least the most vocal protagonists in these matters, in the schools. Because the schools are compulsory to the whole population, and because the whole population can hardly be called radical since they still vote as a majority for the Labour and Conservative parties, it is not surprising that the most radical attempts seen in higher education failed to spread into the schools in spite of one or two episodes. For the most part, teacher radicalism has been concerned with defending the comprehensive system, and with advancing claims of teachers as employed professionals.

In this context, deschooling and free school movements in Britain are more interesting than important. Attempts to deschool, as described by Ivan Illich in *Deschooling Society*, in which pupils will cast off organised education and put together their own educational packages, preferably with the help of computer-run assisted learning systems, are more important for the attack they make on the institutions than for the alternatives they propose. Free schools, on the other hand, are something different. The few that have been created in Britain have not, in fact, deinstitutionalised education but have introduced something approaching a voluntary principle. Pupils who declined to go to other schools were recruited without the normal legal compulsions. They might be regarded more as a voluntary annexe to the main line system rather than as an attempt to overthrow it.

In glancing at these institutive movements since the 1960s in Britain it is too easy to forget what the struggles of previous generations have been about. From the 1900s onwards, radicals in Britain had fought to institutionalise education. They had struggled to ensure that all members of the population would receive education well beyond the ages of five to twelve which was the compulsory period first set in the 1899 Education Act. It never entered their minds that the establishment of a national system of education, albeit locally administered, would so soon fall under the criticism of those who would so quickly cease to rejoice in the benefits of universal suffrage and universal provision. What I earlier described as the atomism of British politics, of the legitimisation of centrifugal forces anxious to provide counter analyses and counter power to those elected through the ballot box, is one of the extraordinary growths in Britain of the last decade. Education, again, was a central forum at which much of this began to happen.

Chapter 6   The Teachers Become Militant

There are deep cleavages of interest corresponding not only to the widely differing standpoints of different interest groups but also to the different perspectives of those who run systems and of those who claim benefits from them. Also, there is the problem discussed in Chapter 4 of precisely what teachers should be expected to produce.

But, as we have seen, 'wider participation' has meant all things to all men, and teachers' demand for participation and power would lead to very different results from those of the ordinary elector and parent. Parents of school children, like users of the post office or public transport, might want more power over those who provide the service. At the same time, however, those who provide the service want a bigger say in the running of it, and a larger share of the collective resource than clients might want to give them. The present government (1977) has attempted to meet both types of demand but has probably most strongly supported those who are employed by the public systems. The leading example to date has been the decision of the government, following the Bullock Report on Industrial Democracy, effectively to denationalise the post office by appointing directors mostly representing not the users but the employed beneficiaries drawn from those who either manage the post office or are nominees of the trade unions representing employees of it.

As the authority of public management systems weakens, so the somewhat deferential attitude of many teachers to their employers can no longer be guaranteed. Previously, individual rights were not well respected. For example, unmarried women teachers who had babies were still being disqualified from teaching for life in the 1920s. The relationship between the more junior teachers and the head ceased to be that of deference and discipline. Informality has increased and with it authoritarianism has declined. The teaching profession was participating in the enormous changes in power between employers and employees, hierarchs and subordinates.

Britain in the 1970s became more acutely aware of the power of the trade unions. That power was demonstrated in many forms. The public sector industrial unions, representing the miners and transport in particular, showed in 1973 and 1974 how they could bring the economy to a halt if their demands were not met. The more remarkable thing about this period is, however, that those whose work was *not* essential, in the sense that the country would not come to a standstill if they went on strike, were also to demonstrate institutional power. This was partly because of the deference of the 1974 Labour Government to the unions and the TUC and partly because methods hitherto regarded as unacceptable or even illegal, such as picketing or sit-ins or mass demonstrations, all became part of the mode of political discourse.

Central and local government have only fallen out with teachers when issues of resources and salaries come to the fore. A sharper form of militancy emerged in the 1960s. The teachers' associations had found themselves facing salaries policies which for a long time favoured the private sector as against some parts of the public sector, although the civil service were notably exempt from the relative deterioration in public service conditions. They had got themselves the Priestley Commission of 1956 which established the concept of comparisons with comparable professions. The school system expanded and with it teaching took on even more the characteristics of a mass profession. Teacher politics became far more sharply unionised and politicised. The National Association of School Masters, a right wing and a 'red necked' body, originally concerned mainly with opposing equal pay for women teachers, as early as 1961 brought out teachers on strike for the first time in three decades. One by one the teacher associations followed each other into the Trade Union Congress. The National Association of School Masters was the first in 1961. All the other associations, except the Joint Four Secondary Associations, traditionally the bastion of grammar and public school teachers, joined, including the Association of University Teachers in 1976.

One commentator on teacher politics has given an explanation for this growing unionisation. David Coates, in *Teachers' Unions and Interest Group Politics* (1972), argues that when the education service found that educational salaries were becoming more subject to general government policies, it became aware of its ineffectiveness arising from DES subordination to the Treasury and the Ministry of Labour or its successors, in any discussion of its demands.

There is certainly something in this thesis, but, in the view of this author, it tends to underestimate the extent to which the Ministry of Education has always been subordinate to Treasury instructions on public sector salaries. What has happened is that there are now more systematic salary policies which are more overtly prescribed by the Treasury. They had been prescribed just as strongly in the past but the Treasury had been more discreet in its dominance of the departments concerned with public sector manpower and salaries. The more significant movement is that of teacher attitudes and of those of all public employees.

Teacher expectations reached a high point in 1974 when Heath's Conservative Government was broken, not by the wage earners of private industry, but by those in such publicly owned services as the mines, the railways and the electricity power industry. Teachers, too, put great pressure on the Labour Government and in the Houghton Committee's report of January 1975 suddenly found themselves, with other parts of public service, in the money. At this point, some of the teachers' leaders took on the postures and the colouring of the more radical politics of other mass professions. This book does not attempt to cover Scottish

3

politics but it must be noted that the language and tactics of the Scottish teachers' union's campaign during the Houghton Committee's sitting was raucous, unreflecting about the general good, and to some extent successful in bullying an already sympathetic government. The committee recommended an average of 29 per cent increase for school and further education teachers, ranging from 47 per cent for polytechnic principals to 15·7 per cent for newly recruited teachers. Throughout the committee's meetings, the main Scottish union, the Educational Institute of Scotland, disrupted the schools by a series of three day strikes and they, in the opinion of some, affected the examination prospects of many pupils. They were thus attempting to influence a committee in session and they certainly managed to get its chairman and some ministers into a tizzy.

These demands from a hitherto underpaid and respectable profession were, then, part of the unionisation and politicisation of the education service. As such, the teachers responded to the general mood. Government had hitherto referred to a 'partnership' between central and local government, and the teachers. This rhetoric now weakened.

Now education was coming into a far more combative period in which strike action and militancy became an important mode of expression and in which the formalised negotiations could no longer be relied upon as binding on the main partners. Teachers came out on strike in London very many times between 1974 and 1977.

They were worried about cuts in the education service and in the reduction of employment possibilities for teachers. As in all such protests, the motives were mixed. Cuts in the education service mean cuts in promotion prospects and increases in, or failure to decrease, the size of classes. They were thus protesting on behalf of their clientele as well as of their own employment interests. There were other motives too. Support for teachers subjected to disciplining by employers was also a recurrent theme.

The mood not only affected the unions but also intra-union relationships. Within the National Union of Teachers, until the early 1960s the mass union of the teaching profession, the Rank and File movement demanded more teacher power in the schools and more militancy in negotiating with the authorities. They were opposed to salaried hierarchies within the school system as well as to what were considered, until 1974, the low salaries paid to teachers. At each point they challenged the leadership of the National Union of Teachers. And similar attitudes began to spread elsewhere. The National Union of School Students demanded more power for students within the schools as well as an end to some of the more trivial manifestations of discipline.

At the same time as teachers became more militant, junior hospital doctors had taken industrial action as a protest against their low pay and conditions and they, like industrial workers, were granted payment for overtime work. In the summer of 1977, a British Medical Association Conference decided that GPs and consultants would take industrial action if their salary claims in defiance of the Phase II arrangements were not met. In other words, we see in the 1970s how the teachers, with many other publicly employed professions, including, it must be noted, all but the more senior grades of the civil service, were prepared to shed the dignified restraints of professionals and become militant in their demands for an equal share of resources.

Chapter 7 Education Goes to Law

A sure indication of the break-up of consensus was the way in which the authority of the Secretary of State and of local authorities was challenged in the courts in two major cases between 1967 and 1976. The parents of Enfield in Middlesex took their local authority to law in an attempt to save a grammar school. The Tameside local authority fought a Labour Secretary of State in the courts to which he brought them because they would not accept his ruling under the Education Act that their attempt to reverse a system of comprehensive education was 'unreasonable'. The Inner London Education Authority did not take teachers to court, but established their own quasi-legal tribunal in order to deal with the troubles of the William Tyndale Junior School in Islington, London.

In the past, it would have been unlikely that these issues would have reached the point where it seemed necessary to have an open test of strength. The system could consume its own smoke. Like the first Elizabethans, the British are becoming more litigious. Objectors now act either militantly or by challenging decisions forensically.

In 1967, the Enfield local authority was challenged by rate-payers and parents (Bradbury *v* Enfield LBC) on a scheme of reorganisation affecting 28 secondary schools. In the case of 20 of the 28 schools, the local authority published notice of intention under Section 13 of the Education Act 1944 to create 'new schools' (that is, changing formerly selective and non-selective schools into comprehensive schools), but went ahead without waiting for the minister's approval of plans required by the Standards for School Premises Regulations, 1959, or any direction from him waiving certain prescribed standards. The Court of Appeal held that under the

Education Act the only channel of complaint was to the minister himself and there was no redress in the courts.

But in the case of eight schools, including a boys' grammar school, where no notices of intention to change the character of the school were issued because the authority and the minister did not think that the changes amounted to 'ceasing to maintain' the existing schools, the Court of Appeal took a different view. It restrained the minister's and local authorities' exercise of authority until the whole procedure of publishing notices had been gone through and the minister had approved the proposals.

A second action concerned Enfield Grammar School alone and is important in terms of our theme of the politics of change because it was not brought by a group of parents of boys at the school and this was, indeed, one of the points advanced by the defence. A wider political group was formed to 'defend' the school. In Lee *v* Enfield LBC (1967) an injunction was granted to restrain the Enfield Borough Council and the school governors from replacing the selective intake of 11 + students with a 'mixed entry' scheme on the grounds that this admissions procedure was contrary to the articles of government of the school. A further action then took place and a declaration was granted against the Secretary of State for giving objectors only five days to object to the revised admission proposals, made by altering the articles of government, on the grounds that this was unreasonable and a denial of statutory rights.

The Education Act of 1968 was passed to widen the Secretary of State's discretion over what amounts to a change of character of a school, stating that changes in arrangements for admission by reference to age, sex, ability or aptitude are to be regarded as a change of character. The regulations relating to the submission of plans were loosened.

This case demonstrates important factors at work. Parents were showing that they could organise themselves both politically and forensically. For the first time, too, national Conservative politicians seemed willing to advise parents how to resist the policies of a Labour government and local authority. Their counsel, Geoffrey Howe, QC, later became the Conservative Attorney General and Shadow Chancellor of the Exchequer. Parent power was now able to move from talking and pamphleteering about the general issues of standards and participation, as such bodies as the Confederation for the Advancement of State Education had done for some years, towards taking expensive, technically sophisticated and politically tough actions against elected councils and the DES.

The Enfield case demonstrated a change of general, if not legal, understandings about the right of the Secretary of State and the local authorities to determine educational issues. The point of view upheld by the courts was that parents had a right to be protected against abuse of power and discretion. It was not the substance of the local authorities' decision but the way in which they and the DES sought to administer it which the courts disliked.

But in the view of two experts on school government (G. Baron and D. A. Howell; see their book *The Government and Management of Schools*, 1973) the judgment can be criticised as excessively narrow in its implications for substance. Some of their criticisms refer to the failure of the judges, in the third of the cases (Lee *v* DES, 1967), to take account of the fact that a local education authority is required to provide a full and sufficient range of schools catering for pupils of all ranges of age, ability and aptitude. Articles of government are only one of a number of relevant provisions in the 1944 Act, and the judges' attention was concentrated almost exclusively on the formal provisions of these. The courts, they say, took virtually no account of the actual rather than formal relationship between the governing body and the local authority. If the precise requirements of the statute had to be complied with so that working to the legal rule was the overriding principle without due weighting of any one legal requirement, the education service might well grind to a halt and the object of the law be forfeited.

None of these actions by the courts would surprise lawyers. The education service, however, was not used to seeing its administrative judgments subjected to parental challenges and legal scrutiny of this order.

The Tameside episode was an even more dramatic challenge to ministerial authority. The local authority had prepared schemes for converting all secondary schools into comprehensive schools. In February 1976, however, the Conservatives were returned to power in Tameside council, partly, it is alleged, on the somewhat contentious evidence of declining standards in nearby Manchester's comprehensive schools.

The councillors promptly reversed their predecessors' plans and attempted to reintroduce selection for secondary school pupils. The Secretary of State deemed them to be acting 'unreasonably' under Section 76 of the Education Act and ordered them to revert to the scheme already approved. They refused and the Secretary of State sought an order of mandamus in the Divisional Court to order the authority to comply with his letter of directive. This was granted but reversed by the Court of Appeal and the Secretary of State then lost his final appeal to the House of Lords. The Law Lords considered that Fred Mulley, the Secretary of State, had failed to 'direct' himself adequately on the feasibility and hence the reasonableness of the Tameside selection scheme: it could not be said that the authority was acting in a way in which no reasonable authority would have acted, and this was the test the courts said had to be applied.

The role played by the courts is consistent with a general trend towards testing the discretion granted ministers by legislation. But, hitherto, ministers of education had not hesitated to declare local authorities to be acting unreasonably under Section 68 of the Education Act on matters where the layman might think that there was a straight difference of opinion on merits as between the minister and the local authority. In the past, for example, they have directed local authorities not to reduce nursery class places, which Somerset did in response to an economy circular, or to impose a closed shop for teachers (Durham) or to require retirement of teachers reaching the age of sixty (Merthyr Tydfil) or to provide education for a handicapped child in a special school instead of an ordinary class (Cheshire). The case of Tameside, however, will very likely make the Secretary of State more cautious in using his powers to direct. The Secretary of State claimed to have acted because the scheme for halting comprehensivisation seemed to him to be administratively unfeasible within the limited time available. But the judges said that he could give a valid direction only if he were satisfied that no reasonable local authority could have decided as the Conservative majority did; and that he could not have been so satisfied. In the opinion of Professor John Griffith (see his book in this series, *The Politics of the Judiciary*, Chapter 5) the minister had sound administrative reasons for his direction but the judges held them to be insufficient.

Whether or not previous ministers have been right in using their powers to direct local authorities is not the issue here. Nor need we be concerned with whether the courts were making a competent construction of the law. John Griffith's view is that the courts' interpretation of the way in which judges review ministers' discretion is that 'the courts interpret such phrases so as to give themselves more or less control as they wish'. 'And one is often left with the feeling that in this area of the law judges rely almost entirely on their own sense of justice or on their own, personal conception of what is best.' To the layman it seems that if the judges are requiring a Labour minister only to intervene on a test of unreasonableness with which Conservative councils would agree, they are restricting his ability to take into balance the desirability of a move in a particular ideological direction as against his view of what is feasible or not feasible on administrative grounds.

The important issue is, however, that whilst we may be far away from the position of the United States courts where social science information is taken into account and the predictions of the social consequences of a judgment argued in detail, in education, at least, the courts will become an arena for the debate of issues of policy, whether or not they are presented as questions of procedure. What had hitherto been a closed system in which the minister acted in judgment over what he deemed to be reasonable or unreasonable actions of authorities will now be open to judicial process. That could always have happened. But the judges have only now been triggered off to act in this way in education. The same trend may be reinforced by the legislation on race relations and equal opportunities for both sexes which also requires the courts to determine intentions on information and opinions submitted to them by publicly appointed and funded commissions.

These issues were, then, challenged in, if not resolved by the courts. The issues, however, brought out into the open by the William Tyndale Junior and Infant Schools Public Inquiry were a result of strong public pressure on the ILEA and taken up by its own tribunal system. In 1976, after 63 days of hearing of evidence, during which time the managers and several others had legal representation costing £50,000, Robin Auld, QC, produced a 309-page report (excluding appendices) on the conduct of a small junior school in Islington. The inquiry brought into the open several themes which illuminate the landscape of educational politics like flashes of lightning. Here was a small group of teachers who were determined to create a school in which the distance and difference between teacher and pupil should virtually disappear, in which teachers should be free to work out their own educational philosophy without control or 'interference' from the local authority appointed managers. By all accounts, except for those of the teachers committed to this course of action and a minority of the parents, the results were disastrous. Some of them are suavely indicated in the reports of the ILEA inspecting team:

> A particular problem appears to be over children who wander, even sometimes disappearing altogether ... To the head misbehaviour in school is primarily a reaction to outside influences. If a child comes late, it is not he who is necessarily to blame. If obscenities are used in the home we may expect obscene language from the child ... There is perhaps no clear lead in the school—the head may not want a lead. The fervour of some staff may have led inexperienced teachers out of their pedagogical depth. (Auld Report, Appendix XV, pages 6 and 7.)

The inquiry found that the teaching organisation, content and quality of teaching, and the discipline of the school were all poor, the latter to the point where it was causing serious and increasing disruption of the infants' school sharing the same building. Collective decision-making in the school had broken down. The head and some of the staff had lost the confidence of the managers and of many parents. Educational policies had been introduced that were badly planned and implemented, and in some cases plainly impracticable.

The report, which is absorbing reading throughout, comes to some striking conclusions. The first is that though a local authority might transfer control of the conduct of the curriculum to the headmaster, subject to the 'oversight' of managers, it must intervene if the school fails to produce adequate education. So a school and its teachers have freedom but not autonomy. The head is in effective control of the school. The managers have a vaguely stated power to 'oversee' the school which is normally construed as 'consultation'. But when this vague relationship between managers and head breaks down, the managers must act corporately, in consultation with the head, by sending the resolution to the local authority.

The case has enormous implications. It shows, first of all,

how teachers have power to go to extreme forms of doctrine and practice before the governing system can check them. This must be borne in mind when accountability systems are considered. The ILEA, for all of its large and experienced inspectorate, seemed incapable of acting effectively for a long while against teacher power. Secondly, it demonstrates one of the extreme positions of doctrine, of pupil autonomy and participation, discussed in Chapter 3. In this case, the teachers mainly involved were particularly taken up with assumptions about how to educate children from poor families. They thought it important to disregard 'middle-class' or even 'pushy working-class' anxieties and values. Thirdly, it demonstrates how parental discontent can cause criticisms to be converted into action. The William Tyndale parents were lucky in having sophisticated social democratic councillors who could take up the issue and pursue it even if, according to the chairman of the inquiry, they sometimes used procedures that were open to criticism.

Tyndale demonstrated several conflicts. It showed how largely working-class parents were concerned to get a systematic education as against the more esoteric offerings of extreme 'progressivism' for their children. It showed how there can be conflict between politically appointed managers who have some reason to claim to represent society, since they are appointed by those elected for membership of the GLC and hence the ILEA, as against the claims of teacher freedom and professionalism and their right to determine curriculum and organisation. It also shows the potential power of the client and the consumer to challenge the government if it feels that services are not minimally competent. From the teachers' point of view, as the report says (paragraph 859),

In persisting with their defiance of the authority to the extent of going on strike rather than being inspected, the junior school staff demonstrated how much importance they attached to the inviolability of their 'professional status' and how little thought they had for the children for whose education they were responsible.

A further question is whether education's review system is adequate. It could be said that Tyndale was an exceedingly painful expression and cumbersome way of correcting poor work in a school.

In bringing issues of educational policy before the courts, or out into the open as through the William Tyndale Inquiry, the main actors were not creating new boundaries or concepts for legal action. But the increased activity in itself was symptomatic of two major changes. The first was the refusal of different groups affected by radical changes in educational policy to accept the decisions theoretically made for them by the democratically appointed politicians. So once they had lost the issue on merits (inasmuch as their preferred solutions were not endorsed by the majority of the electorate), they sought to frustrate policies by challenges to the ways in which rules were administered. But challenges to the way that rules are administered often entail challenges to substance as well. And, certainly, when the courts begin to examine how hitherto unchallenged parts of the system exercise their judgments on what is reasonable, the kind of information that a Secretary of State brings into his purview before making a political decision, the courts themselves are getting into the substantive issues. From our point of view, we have to reckon with decision-making being affected not only by the relationship between electorate and the formal system they authorise to make decisions but, increasingly, with challenges on procedures as well.

Chapter 8 Curriculum and Authority in Higher Education

The most sophisticated and direct challenges on questions of academic purpose and governance have been launched within higher education.

No university or polytechnic was immune to challenges which related to two propositions. The first argument put up by radicals was that education and knowledge are not so much the product of a specialised training and skill, but are social accretions which have no more validity, and perhaps less relevance, than the thinking of the most recent generation of students, or those who are not students at all but are part of the 'world of work'. The second and linked proposition was that higher education should cease to have the characteristics of institutions marked by the division of labour and should become instead open democracies in which teachers and students count as equal members with an equal voice.

This kind of thinking is superficially similar to the process, adapted by scholars from the work of Karl Popper, known as falsification, in which propositions and categories of knowledge are tested to see whether, and to what extent, they can be changed, improved or discarded by considering whether the opposite of them is conceivable. That process takes some propositions to be scientific inasmuch as their opposite is imaginable and conceivable while calling others merely psychologisms. Some such process which now dominates all reflective research and teaching also assumes that the researcher or student has knowledge of the propositions being tested and has also taken time to acquire skills in argument, logic, conceptualisation and testing.

The authority attributed to acquired knowledge, as

embodied in senates, professors, examining boards and text books, was seriously damaged by criticism which centred round that particular critique known as the Sociology of Knowledge, and by the spreading influence of sociology in general. Works such as *Counter Course*, edited by Trevor Pateman, summed up many of the arguments of critics of the academic system. The sociological critique of education maintained that the curriculum derives from the processes and structures by which it is created. If it is created and authorised by a specialist community of academics, it is likely to carry with it the assumptions of that group. These assumptions will be those of the power group of which they are part, namely the British establishment, tied as it is to a class structure and an employment system and the specialist division of labour. Academics are concerned with the continuity and accretion of knowledge which, at least in the Marxist version of the argument, rests on selectively created views of society and power. The radical view regards knowledge as derived from continuously changing perspectives of the groups in society whose place in the knowledge-creation industry has been 'expropriated' by the academic establishment. Note here the utopian flavour. There was, it seems, a golden age in which institutions which oppressed the majority did not exist, and there will be a golden age in which wicked institutions will wither away. Then each generation of students, and the larger society from which they spring, will have no lower place in the hierarchy of knowledge generators than do, say, university teachers. From this notion, of course, sprang the demand that higher education should be open to all irrespective of initial qualifications.

It follows from these arguments that examinations administered by teachers are not true validations of knowledge because that which they test consists of socially generated and biased constructions of reality. The examinations themselves are seen as coercive and potentially punitive exercises administered for the sake of control and for maintaining the power of teachers. These arguments, lodged with different intensities by different groups, and accepted or rejected by academic systems with varying degrees of over- and under-reaction, constituted the intellectual justification for many institutional changes. No British university admitted a student majority to its course boards, as did some universities in Denmark, Holland and West Germany. But all admitted representatives of students to the main academic bodies, university councils, senates and course boards, within higher education other than those concerned with the appointment of staff (save, apparently for one or two exceptions when vice-chancellors were being appointed) or examining boards. Student criticism certainly helped change the hitherto rigidly administered examination systems and advance notice questions and project work assumed an important place in examination systems. Student unions became, in effect, a publicly sanctioned and financed counter-institution in many of the establishments of which they became part. Student politicians, most of them on publicly financed sabbatical leaves, became full-time bureaucrats responsible for a wide range of activities often offered in place of or in competition with those traditionally thought to be part of the university's pastoral and tutorial systems.

That the student demands for participation had an effect on higher education is beyond doubt. They came at a time when higher education had moved from providing for an elite of 3·2 per cent in university and perhaps a further 2·6 per cent in other higher courses in 1954 to something approaching mass higher education providing degree courses for perhaps 13 per cent of the age group. The changes certainly forced teachers to think about their role in society and their relationships with students. They forced discussion on many issues which had too comfortably lain dormant for decades. At the same time, many teachers, and others outside the universities and polytechnics, could not fail to be appalled by the violence of some of the actions taken by some student leaders in the late 1960s when, in a few cases, teachers were physically assaulted. The use of sit-ins, which is a physical form of coercion, seemed to be regarded as an ordinary means of discourse. A period which regarded spontaneity and reappraisal of received doctrines as the commonplace could not accept as well the need for stability and personal self-respect among those whom student leaders attacked. Those of us who have been the targets of student attack in our own institutions will know how thoroughly demoralising strong and public accusation based on mis-understood information can be, and how destructive it is of both the work for which teachers are appointed and reason-able working relationships with students.

Again, however, education was both participating in and forming part of the general changes in modes of social behaviour and political action. The picket line, the massive retaliation against grievance, the insistence on equality of participation irrespective of disparities of function, all were features of Britain from the 1960s onwards.

New notions have emerged which do not start with assumptions about the intellectual or scientific process so much as feelings about what ought to happen in society. Thus, the fact that the female moiety and racial minorities have been deprived of opportunities in the past is certainly a moral issue which has needed attention. The fact that this has happened in the past is also a matter of historical interest, and the fact that ascriptions of roles are applied differentially now is also a matter of sociological and psychological interest, and of legitimate political conflict. The response of some teachers has been to introduce such subjects as 'women's studies' or 'black studies', which could start with propositions and facts to be tested and to be improved on, but can also start with statements of grievances to be expounded. Some student bodies, with the help of some teachers, seek to set up alternative courses on the assumption that, for example, sociologists teaching deviance may not be trusted to produce a sufficiently wide or dissenting range of opinions on the subject.

At this point in time, it is difficult for the committed observer to be fair to some of these changes. Academic progress has always depended on the reiterative challenges embodied in processes of falsification, as just described, which constitute intellectual due process. It has also, in the past, benefited from quite violent attacks on established beliefs and procedures. The emancipation of philosophy and science from primitive medieval dogma was, at least in part, the product of new ways of thinking (the dialectic of Abelard in the twelfth century, the exploitation of Aristotelian thinking by Thomas Aquinas in the thirteenth and the logical scepticism of William of Ockham in the fourteenth century); it was also partly the result of new teaching methods which strongly countered the orthodoxies of the official universities. The study of minorities and what they need may as well start from a study of perceived problems rather than attempt to make a more 'objective' and comprehensive analysis of all of the components without any directional thesis upon which the study can be based.

Moreover, students of higher education have increasingly followed many school teachers in emphasising the need for treating higher education as important in terms of the processes rather than the products that it induces. That is to say, since knowledge is, by whatever doctrine, the result of a continuing process of change or falsification, and of confirmation, followed by testing and further change, it is the ability to undergo that process and not to produce set categories of knowledge that should be important. It is certainly too easy for teachers at all levels to stick to that which reassures because of its familiarity. Whatever their faults, radical students have made it virtually impossible for teachers to persist in that type of error.

From these assumptions follow quite plain consequences in terms of educational governance. Where they triumph, the authority of teachers and examiners becomes suspect. Institutions become deprived of their specialist status and, it

96

is argued, should cease to be governed and controlled by those who have command of specialist skills. They might become instead community centres or youth cities, as one American professor of philosophy, John Searle, writing of the attempt by radicals to smash the university at Berkeley, California, described it in *The Campus War*.

All of these social changes and changes in attitudes towards authority have affected the way in which higher education works. Its authority rests on its assumed functions. For example, examiners in universities were always assumed to have absolute authority in reaching individual judgments, in much the same way as does a jury sitting in a court of law. They ensured that society's elite was authoritatively licensed because the skill and knowledge of graduates were attested by those in a position to do so. The appointment of staff has always been assumed to be the subject of professional decisions taken in camera but according to due process. Both of these sets of procedures have been challenged by some students and university teachers who believe that judgment-making should be universal rather than exclusive to those who have hitherto been assumed to have earned the right to be deemed competent.

The results of these changes in feelings in the society have, then, fed into the newly expanded higher education system which, in its turn, has reinforced and promulgated changes of social belief about educational exclusivity and the rights and power of highly selected university teachers and researchers to establish the norms of logic and of credibility. The resulting change in ethos must be unbelievable to anybody who received their education in a traditional university before, say, 1955. The social ethos of the changes has been brilliantly documented in such accounts of British universities as David Lodge's *Changing Places*, Malcolm Bradbury's *The History Man* or C. P. Snow's account of Cambridge in the late 1960s, *Last Things*. The mood was expressed in surely one of the most idiotic fad books of the period, Charles Reich's *The Greening of America* (1970) in which the author stressed the importance of university professors wearing bellbottom trousers so as to reduce their pompous claims to authority. (Some university professors do wear bellbottom trousers. Surely there is room for a mordant study, perhaps to be reported in *New Society*, of the effect of them doing so.) Institutions and authority came under attack. Reciprocally, there was a surge of concern for many groups whom the system had hitherto seemed to ignore: racial and sexual minorities; a belief in and commitment to voluntary action on behalf of those in need; a more passionate involvement in issues of world poverty and politics; all of these grew as did the reduction in confidence in the publicly maintained structure.

Changes in higher education have been well analysed by an American sociologist, Martin Trow, whose article 'Problems in the Transition from Elite to Mass Higher Education' (1963) describes three stages in the development of higher education. The first, which we are now passing, is the elite stage: universities were able to observe certain norms; for example, an academic was morally committed to give academic help to any fellow academic within his own institution, irrespective of the discipline. (How far all met that obligation is, of course, another matter.) Also, an academic was required to give help to an academic from his own field from any other university within the world. Moreover, and this is not explicitly stated by Trow, he was expected to pay attention to the work being done elsewhere. He was thus master of his own discipline in the sense that my own tutor was able to say to me in 1951 that he had read everything that had ever been written about eighteenth-century Britain.

As far as the expected behaviour of the student body was concerned, the fact that they were an elite chosen overtly for academic excellence but also for leadership potential meant that they were, in effect, opting into an apprenticeship to a society where the norms were both academic and social. Trow's second stage, the move to mass education, produces considerable changes. By mass higher education he means a point reached where, perhaps, 15 per cent of an age group can expect to go on to higher education. And where higher education becomes universal (the third stage), that is to say, all students with minimum qualifications may expect a place, even more serious structural consequences follow. Academics can no longer respond to the norms stated for them in the elite system because there are too many colleagues with whom they must relate. And as higher education plant expands, so does its output in terms of what must be read and mastered. The institutions do indeed take on some of the characteristics of youth cities. Students do not reckon to join an apprenticeship in which teachers are deemed to have mastery of disciplines which they will pass on to the willing young but are, instead, part of a complicated system of individual rights. In this a student is entitled, as is the pensioner, the sick or any other client group of the Welfare State, to continue in membership on terms which are set as much by the prevailing moods of the student body as by the more continuous if narrow norms of the academic community.

So, changes in access cause changes in expectations and they also cause changes in structure. For as British higher education has moved into the mass stage and hovers on the brink of universality, so the power of the academic system has been reduced, the authority of scholarship has been damaged and the power of consumerism has grown. Such major figures in British society as vice-chancellors and at least some professors have become typified not as spokesmen of a continuing culture and tradition of learning but as part of a fairly esoteric management system.

At the same time, public moods towards higher education changed. There used to be a love affair between Whitehall and the universities which enabled the Treasury to give free monies through the Universities Grants Committee on the assumption that good work would follow. In this the universities were indistinguishable from the Old Vic or the National Gallery. But now the new accountability mood has caused Whitehall to try, not to define what is meant by good work, but to require academics to show—without, however, stating its own views—what it thinks they ought to do. The ideas have to be justified by their context of usefulness or of meeting demand as well as in their quality. Moreover, the number of tenured academics in universities has grown until it is now something like 24,000. At one time there were not many more academics than there were members of the administrative civil service (3000) and the reciprocal feelings of eliteness were at that time easier to accept.

Since 1966, the universities have been subject to public audit as if they were any part of the public system. The quinquennial system of grants by which the universities were given freedom in five-year dollops in return for meeting the most general of prescriptions from Whitehall has given way, temporarily it is said, to a jerking, spasmodic and unsystematic award of grant annually. Universities, built up at a time when expansion seemed to be a continuing responsibility, now find themselves half completed; also, partly because they have never been allowed to mature in public favour, they are finding it difficult in some years to recruit students. The polytechnics, so loudly proclaimed as the doers of public good, are even weaker than some of the newer universities, even though placed in a position of parity by the awards of the Houghton Committee which gave them more than equal pay with their university counterparts. Pressure for places has gone down. Able youths seek alternative ways both to employment and to intellectual status. Unemployment put the figures up in 1977 but the long-term movement is unclear.

The universities have experienced every twist and turn of political fortunes. They exemplify the way in which free charter institutions are increasingly subjected to public prescriptions. They exemplify the way in which government is uncertain of its objectives and, instead of leaving things alone, visits that uncertainty on the objects of its administration. They have faced, with particular uncertainty and corresponding ferocity from their protagonists, the attacks from consumerism. They face demands for control by the beneficiaries of public money who wish to take them over, through the student unions and through political groups. They thus face attacks on the authority of knowledge and tradition from the radical left, and conservative attacks from those who want public bodies to be accountable to public systems.

In this story of declining fortunes we see how education expanded, and thus gave much more to many people and at less cost. We also have seen how social trends ceased to allow institutions to be confident of their own traditions whilst new counter institutions emerged. The Open University, for example, has most successfully countered the assumptions that good university education needs to be residential, that traditional entry qualifications are essential, and that face-to-face encounter is necessarily better than educational technology. The growth of student unions is a subject of study in its own right, and not simply at the polemical level of university teachers dismayed at some of the more extreme manifestations of strident student union bureaucracies. In many respects they represent attempts to create new institutions for youth and run by youth and as such have positive elements of welfare and of social coherence which cannot be ignored.

These movements in educational governance have a strong bearing on how the country is governed, and on what criteria. They reflect movements well beyond the educational domain. If society has no validated and useful stock of concepts, facts, attitudes and values to pass on, such concepts as that of 'due process', with its belief that agreements should not be lightly dislodged in favour of new and untested ones, become at a discount. If, on the contrary, education is seen as a stock of transmittable skills and facts as well as an individualised progress to personal power and understanding, it follows that government and the employment system can hope to hold the schools accountable for producing the types of manpower they think they need. If the new elites are educated within a do-it-yourself framework, it follows that authority in the larger society will equally well be diffused and up for recurrent tests, if not for permanent revolution.

Chapter 9   Equality

The last of the important themes of concern to the education service during our period was that of equality. We have already described how the soft gave way to the hard concept of equality. In the immediate post-war period, the able could get to the top of an elite selective system. Under the 'hard' concept the most deprived will get proportionately more to enable them to advance. In secondary education, as we have shown in Chapter 2, the 1944 Act attempted to do away with the grossest inequalities by making secondary education available to all.

The 1944 Act did a remarkably revolutionary thing, although it is no longer fashionable to say so. It turned post-primary education, that is education from the age of eleven, into a system in which comparisons could be made. All schools were to be called 'secondary', a term hitherto reserved for the elite parts of the maintained system. Eventually, everybody was to stay in school until sixteen. All pupils were to have access to GCE (and, later, CSE) courses, although the curriculum was designed only for the ablest 40 per cent. In this situation, the result is not one of 'strong' equality. 'Parity of esteem' or 'democratisation' (the equivalent French term) simply made the in-built inequalities more obvious to a population that wanted far more than the secondary modern schools could offer. So the soft concept of equality, in which all would start equal in the race whether nimble-footed or lame and halt, gave way to the hard concept of equality where the starts would be staggered. But to do this, it was argued, all must be in the same race-track— the comprehensive school. And since the Newsom Report (1963), with its 'each child must be allowed to improve his intelligence', and the Plowden Report (1967), with its educational priority areas, primary and secondary schools whose population were deprived would receive extra resources of staff, buildings and money so as to equalise results and not simply equalise opportunities.

The same impulses are moving through higher education. As we have already noticed, the system has moved from elitism to mass higher education and the demands are increasing that it become universal, through the provision of adult education that would lead to the creation of a comprehensive tertiary system.

Between 1950/1 and 1975/6 students in advanced degree courses in universities rose from 69,000 in universities and a far smaller number in the non-university sector to some 435,000 in both private and public sectors. The non-advanced further education sector had nearly two million places in 1975. By the time expansion had finished there were thirty new polytechnics in England and Wales, ten new universities created from the former colleges of advanced technology and the creation of major new universities such as Sussex, York, Lancaster, Essex and Warwick—an increase from twenty-four to forty-four in the 1960s. The educational landscape had radically changed.

Many of the ideological issues concerned with these changes have already been traced. Our concern here will be to note how social engineering, the attempt to cause changes in the social structure and in social relationships, interacts with such a system as education.

In the 1960s two aspects of social relativity became dominant in educational thinking. If it is insufficient to equalise opportunity because not all can take advantage of it, there must be positive discrimination. It is argued that planners must give more to the seriously deprived than to their better-off fellows. But the concept of relative deprivation tells us that as standards rise, so do the legitimate aspirations of all recipients of social goods. There is thus an endless progression to be financed and provisioned which can only end when all have equal ability.

The arguments against inequality, and attempts to reduce it, become stronger as more people's expectations are raised. At the same time, however, so does the backlash against egalitarianism become stronger. Witness the reaction against the comprehensive schools which we are now experiencing. Moreover, there might be a limit to the number of new doctrines which people can take. The attempt to complete the two stages of egalitarianism, the soft and hard, virtually simultaneously, perhaps was too difficult for society to assimilate within twenty years.

An endless dialectic thus sets in and at no time is it possible to deny two equally valid propositions: that the poor are getting relatively poorer, because they cannot keep up with the advances of the whole economy; and that the highly motivated and potentially successful are having to put a greater proportion of their product into continuing equalisation programmes. This dialectic is complicated even more when certain powerful groups in the society, particularly the unions representing publicly owned industry, are able to get what they ask without much heed to the two sides of the main ideological argument: atomism and syndicalism do not pay much attention to social theory. And all of these themes become hopelessly entangled when the country encounters economic blizzards of the ferocity experienced over the last five years.

The theme of relativity, of not being satisfied with new advances in equality because logically nothing can be enough, is now joined by a second argument which is better christened 'indeterminacy'. Indeterminacy is despair over the inability of social engineering to do anything well. Comprehensive schools are too big, it is argued, although the bigness was an attempt to create mass resources for the whole of the community. New universities and polytechnics are squalid, although far better than their French or Italian equivalents, and costly enough anyway. Mass access to higher education means wider discontent rather than satisfaction. Planning has become the butt of sophisticated political science and economics, as potently attacked by such American neo-conservatives as Charles E. Lindblom, David Braybrooke and Aaron Wildavsky. Indeterminacy, a refusal to be certain about the future and to plan for it other than in an incremental, intuitive and gradualist way, became a fashionable mode, and in curious political alliance with those who dislike institutionalism whilst believing in immediate and non-gradualistic change.

Both of these changes in mood seriously affected British egalitarianism, particularly when educational costs thrust upward at the very time when Britain's economy was in danger.

But even more subtle sets of complications emerge. The British Welfare State is a set of policies and mechanisms largely designed to ensure that minimum living standards reach all of the people and, if in differing degrees, that equality is increasingly achieved. Yet the dispensers of welfare services, including education, have their own value systems and their own technologies which may ultimately conflict with egalitarianism.

We might know what people want, but cannot know how to meet their wishes and needs. We cannot predict the effects of well intentioned, benign and expensive policies any more easily than we can predictively know how to attract and retain the affection and trust of our children or friends. The borderline between helping and condescension, between providing for needs and stigmatising, is thin.

The conflicts became relevant in the educational priority areas, and the doctrine of positive discrimination underlying them proved difficult not only to put into operation and to evaluate but also to reconcile with teacher professionalism. The educational priority areas (EPAs) were devised by the Plowden Committee, and had also been proposed in a different form by the Newsom Committee, in 1967 and 1963 respectively, as ways of reinforcing education for the deprived. The argument ran that since those who came from poor homes could not break out of the cycle of poverty and deprivation because they performed badly at school, it was necessary greatly to enhance their education. With the EPAs, the doctrine of positive discrimination came into effect, for the intention was to give better to those in most need rather than simply to provide equal chances for them. The type of policies which the Plowden Committee recommended included better staffing ratios, better buildings, more money for teachers in the EPA schools, and specific teacher education related to the needs of disadvantaged children.

Attempts were made to create educational priority areas but they have encountered several difficulties. One group of difficulties has been the apparent inability of education to offset the heavy weight of social disadvantage created by poor homes, low expectations of education within the family and peer groups, and low expectations of good employment afterwards. But, secondly, the notion of positive discrimination which seemed so self-evidently right in the mid and late 1960s encountered many of the problems of all attempts to change individual destinies through social engineering. Teachers were not happy with many of the proposals contained in the EPA notion. Attempts, for example, to try out some of the operant conditioning techniques associated with the American Head-start Programmes were seen as inimical to the best that the primary schools could do, even when they were used for strictly testing and experimental purposes. Operant conditioning was introduced in New York schools to help children who came from backgrounds which are unknown even in our worse-off areas. Black children in Harlem had reached the schools not only unable to read, but without any notion of a daily routine involving the telling of time or responding to other social conventions. Teachers feared that educational priority schools would involve rote learning, pre-set procedures which would be contradictory to the liberal educational procedures and principles so strongly endorsed by the educational system. Again, teachers felt that to call a school 'deprived' might be to label it, and the children in it. Conventional teacher wisdom said that teachers receiving special allowances for work in such a school might be attracted to the work for the wrong reason, namely, money.

The difficulty of meeting the demands for equality without condescension and without disfunctional stigma and labelling underlie the attempts to create alternative approaches to education. Schooling is not the only form of education. We have already noted the attempts by Illich and many others to propose or create alternatives to it. The Free School movement in Britain has tried, in line with traditions set up much earlier, but mainly by middle-class liberals such as Bertrand Russell or as in A. S. Neill's school, Summerhill, to liberate schooling from its more oppressive and bureaucratic characteristics. The accounts of these attempts certainly highlight the difficulty of providing what individuals need on the mass level. Providing for a school population that has varied between six million and nine million is not an easy or an inexpensive business. Individuation within it is virtually impossible. The reactions to a mass product are understandable and many teachers, in their working relations with pupils, can deinstitutionalise schooling through the methods and relationships that they adopt. But it is not easy.

EQUALITY AND ETHNIC MINORITIES

An important change in British society has been its development into a multi-racial community. The problems of the ethnic communities, and the efforts of the education service to meet them, exemplify some of the issues of defining and combating deprivation. Evidence is mounting that whilst the impact of British society varies greatly as between the different groups, many children from ethnic minorities suffer particularly severe disabilities. They suffer from the general social and work conditions in which their families live, the disparities between the expectations of the longer-settled communities and of those of the more recent arrivals, and difficulties, perhaps resulting from prejudice, of placing minority-group children, and particularly black children, into adequate employment.

The approach of the educational service to these issues has faithfully reflected its more general attitudes towards deprivation. At first, the schools insisted that the best way to help immigrant children was to treat them as if they were not immigrants and to allow them to settle into the schools, to enjoy the individual treatment offered by the best primary schools, and the range of opportunities offered by the secondary schools. In the early 1960s, however, a curious mixture of 'white' parental resentment and of a desire on the part of the education authorities, backed by the DES, to act decisively, led to a policy of positive discrimination, namely, dispersal. So in Southall when the proportion of immigrant children went beyond 30 per cent in the schools, the local authority 'bussed' Asian children. Ealing authority provided what is acknowledged to be excellent English language classes for these children, and has placed them in good schools away from Southall itself where conditions have been cramped and depressing, although the schools are staffed by devoted and able teachers. As we write, some 3000 Asian pupils of primary school age are bussed daily to schools away from Southall. It should be noted, however, that the 30 per cent rule is long abandoned, and in Southall, as elsewhere, there are schools with as many as 90 per cent minority-group children.

Bussing is associated, in the USA, with positively discriminatory policy requiring reactionary school boards to integrate their schools. In Britain, however, it has led to an opinion being expressed by the Race Relations Board that the Southall, or as it now is, Ealing, policy is discriminatory inasmuch as pupils, including those whose native tongue might be English, are dispersed to schools away from Southall where they are thus able to mix with children from the majority groups and thus acquire British 'lore and culture'.

The issues now raised are, in fact, whether children from minority groups should not be allowed to be educated with their own minority, whether the dominant lore and culture should constitute part of the compulsory diet of all children in a multi-racial society, and whether the processes involved in bussing, and selection for it, do not label and hence stigmatise the children. The progressive trend in British education has certainly been against identifying particular problems in this way, as we have already noted.

POSTSCRIPT TO PART TWO

The issues discussed in these last chapters connect with each other. Controversies on the curriculum, attacks on authority, the expansion of higher education, the approaches to law, the attempts at equality and better race relations, have more in common than is at first obvious. It will be convenient here to draw together these themes before looking more closely at the institutions concerned with institutional politics and government.

In all of these cases, there are conflicts between equally legitimate points of view. Egalitarian policies are intended to help the underprivileged, but social engineering seems curiously incapable of doing so in a sufficiently sensitive and non-stigmatising way. Egalitarian policies also mean that the selection of a working elite becomes more difficult. They conflict with professional assumptions about how pupils might be educated.

All of these cases show how there are conflicts between different points of view whenever the education service attempts to move forward. Professionals running the system, the client groups, the radical critics of the system, those who want a larger say in the running of the schools and colleges, all speak to different themes. Small wonder that the political and governing systems of education are complex and reflect much beyond their own scope.

Education in these examples shares the characteristics of all forms of social policy. The basic structure of society has maintained itself even though differentials have become eroded and social relationships sharply altered. The hard concept of equality, the comprehensive schools and educational priority areas, or the moves on race relations, have not abolished inequality and serve to mark out new boundaries of injustice rather than to obliterate them. It has been indicated that there are logical as well as strategic difficulties in making radical change and one of the difficulties has been brilliantly depicted in *Education, Opportunity and Social Inequality* by the French sociologist, Raymond Boudon, who has pointed out, as did the unpublished work of Thomas Green and others, how the social group 'of last entry'—those who are the first generation in a family to have full educational opportunity—have so much further to go before they can begin to compete for the higher levels of educational and social success.

The limited effects of positive action raise fundamental questions about human propensity. Is the education system up against obstinacies in the human condition, or are they artefacts of the social system? Is it possible to provide a distributive system which caters for all and which can yet be sensitive enough to the detailed and individual nature of human needs? The Ealing bussing case is, in fact, a good example of how policy that might have worked extremely well, in terms of the provision being given to individual Asian children, found itself unable to conform to the more general ethic imposed by the law.

These complexities of provision are reflected in the discussion of participation and control. Participative doctrines have attempted to make all of the parties of education into equal democratic units. Teachers with their employment prospects to protect, as well as their schools and profession to advance, parents with individual pupils whose welfare they wish to promote, local authority officials and councillors with a concern for the overall welfare of their constituency as

111

well as their own authority to defend, university teachers with standards to maintain and research to advance, students with the cogent demands of their own generation to expound, all of these comingle in some of the attempts to democratise education.

Current participative doctrine is impatient with differentiations. It demands that all processes should be open and to everybody so that political institutions cannot respect the differences in weighting that educational tasks seem to require.

In the last ten years, the institutions with which most of us have grown up have failed to contain these powerful new simplicities of thinking. Consensus has broken down including the centre theme of Western political democracy that there must be arrangements through which demands can be stated, conflicts resolved and authoritatively settled.

Our society cannot easily adapt its institutions to these changing assumptions. Existing institutional forms and paradigms, of central and local government, of the administration of schools and colleges, which constitute the formal framework, are no longer assumed to mediate adequately and bring together the different groups in society within overriding policies.

The central characteristic of the period that we are discussing is, therefore, that the institutions cannot take all the new political and ideological pressures that are being placed upon them. Changes are not simply those of doctrine, although changes of doctrine have certainly been massive. There are also changes in attitudes within personal relationships and in attitudes towards the larger society.

Were the schools to 'blame' for these attitudinal changes? Certainly, informality had been encouraged in at least a strong minority of primary schools for many decades, though, it must be emphasised, so had a belief in highly motivated work. Whether that informality had spread upwards is doubtful, for increasing disregard of formality and traditional forms was coming from those in society who had never attended post-war British primary schools. One commentator, Harry Ree, attributed it to the traumas of the First World War which he typified in a BBC talk in 1975 as the Death of Dad—the attrition of respect for the older generation which the holocausts of 1914–18 and the fearful economic and social balls-up of 1918–39 had so richly earned. Yet can this be so? For the same mood caught the young everywhere. Those countries relatively untouched by the European war, for example, the USA and Japan, went through precisely the same waves of sentiment. So did countries such as France or Sweden which were barely touched by progressive education. Neither the alleged triumphs of progressive education nor the large-scale social upheavals of fifty years could explain a revolution of attitudes which included the Beatles, the mini-skirt, *That Was the Week That Was*, *Private Eye*, the sit-ins and violence at the LSE and the Polytechnic of North London, the growth of squatting, the Peace Marches, or the establishment of Shelter and the other activist pressure groups.

PART THREE

The Political System

Chapter 10   The Political and Governing Institutions

Introduction

Political institutions generally, but educational systems more particularly, are complex in the ways in which they display tension between continuity and change, consensus and dissent.

As to complexity, we have already seen in the preceding chapters that education has many purposes and many promoters. Its protagonists do not have the single-minded devotion to particular duties of, say, the ICI, or the army, or the RSPCA. Institutional arrangements in education, too, reflect the values and role conflicts of the main stake-holders in education. They reflect multiple purposes for which they are set up, or the purposes which they acquire over time.

As a result, apparently monolithic institutions such as central government departments, the Department of Education and Science (DES), which has existed in one form or the other since the 1840s, or the County Halls in each of the 104 local authorities have to work from multiple concepts of what should be, or is being, governed. Within the controlling system, the elected leaders, the senior officials and specialist professionals such as school inspectors, have different expectations and beliefs about education and about the ways in which it should be administered. Concepts change as different groups of individuals press their claims on the system. So multiple are the concepts, and so potentially conflicting are the claims of different groups, that it is surprising that any change at all takes place for change requires alliances o be forged for long enough for action to occur. That is why consensual policies are often dull and continuous. They are the product of conflicting claims painfully and painstakingly resolved. It is too wearing to change them without good cause. That is why, too, drastic and radical solutions do not work where large scale and long term processes like education are involved. Radical policies in the end have to be reconciled with the inheritance of previous radicalisms.

In Chapters 2 to 8, we showed how many of the disputed issues involved the question of who should have the power to determine educational purposes and content. If the teaching profession is to retain and advance the power which it has for so long enjoyed, teachers have yet to decide through which mechanisms policies should be made. Schools are, in fact, hierarchies, but some want them to be communes or collegia. If the parents should have a larger say, it is unclear whether they can secure it through the traditional ballot-box system, or through the governing bodies which derive their powers from it, or through some other more direct mechanisms. If the national authorities are entitled, by virtue of their parliamentary electoral base, to create national policies for, say, secondary education, they must relate them to the complex web of institutions in which professional power and local government is so strong. And there is uncertainty as to what checks and reviews they might be subject. If students in higher education are effectively to state the needs of future generations, the continuities of science and scholarship need power to remain intact.

All of these issues are 'institutional' and political rather than educational. All of them echo some of the main themes of British politics at large. The role of the unions, of the consumer, of government as against individuals, are all both institutional and substantive matters. They concern fundamental issues of how people can work reliably together on shared purposes and at the same time tolerate, legitimise and accommodate change.

Educational institutions are sources of both continuity and change. They are sources of continuity because of professional power, and even though the school system has been challenged by militancy and consumerism, schools and teachers can hold firm. So, for example, any attempt to force basic skills training, or stronger control or participation by parents, or more progressive forms of education, or their opposite, has to be made not only nationally or in whole local government areas but also in each of some 30,000 schools and colleges, a point James Callaghan seemed not to understand. Whilst schools within areas are quite similar, each is an individual and prime institution able to hold its own.

Moreover, the formal educational policy-making system, the DES in relationship to the local authority associations and teachers' associations, forms a strong system of consensus which provides collective strength. It is true that each side might complain of each other's failure to consult, or to be responsive to consultation. The recent Select Committee inquiry (1976) into the working of the DES referred to 'a widespread feeling that the DES is not sufficiently open in its dealings with the various interest groups involved in education and with the public at large.' (Page xxix, para. 75.)

But over the years, conventions and understandings about the relationships between central government, the local authorities and the schools, about the freedom allowed institutional practitioners, have been confirmed and extended. To outsiders, it is not discussion and lack of consultation so much as cohesion to the point of being a closed system that are the main characteristics of British educational government.

This variety of groups and this supportive tension between central authority and institutional freedom are important to the issues discussed in Chapters 2 to 8, even if ambiguity rather than certainty is exposed when we place the issues in their institutional context.

Against these powerful and consensual continuities there are the components of change. Some changes are created from inside. The momentum for expansion was socially sanctioned, but promoted primarily by the education service. The dominance of the progressive mode in primary education, for example, was internally determined. But, at the same time, external forces, operating largely on the social and economic aspects of education, became enormously strong, particularly as they changed and were thrust forward by the mood of more articulate people, generally on such issues as equality and participation. Educational politics have fermented more vigorously than virtually any other specialised zone of British public activity. No area has experienced or reflected more, the increased range of political activity. Pressure groups, the press, the social science intelligentsia, local politicians, the professionals, local communities, or those who purport to speak for them—the stake-holders and the activists have been particularly important and they have changed rapidly within the thirty years with which we are concerned.

In this chapter, in order to put these complex issues into some order, we will take four arbitrary cut-throughs. First, we will look at the changing patterns of local politics and of the community of which the school is part. Then we will consider the political environment created by national pressure groups. Thirdly, we will look at the role of parliament and the central authorities in education. Finally, we will try to link the changes of central and of local authorities with those which occur at the prime institutional levels.

I: EDUCATION AND LOCAL POLITICS

We start with local politics because education affects individual children and their families at the point at which it all happens, in the schools, maintained, staffed and owned by the local education authorities. The local education authority, which is the county or metropolitan district council, also has many other responsibilities and it is elected every four years. Local politics thus are able to impinge on education in a particularly critical, frequent and complex way.

The local authority determines much of the quality and ethos of education although it does so within general policies laid down by the central government. Central legislation lays down the minimum period of schooling. It has a say on school organisation and on general resource and building levels, through building programmes, through decisions on the supply and distribution of teachers, on whether there should be separate colleges of education, on which institutions should be designated polytechnics, and a host of other important controls.

Yet education is essentially an inter-personal activity between teacher and pupil conducted in individual institutions such as schools and colleges maintained by local authorities.

In the past, local politics have been quiescent about education. No doubt there was more smoke or even flame than is now apparent, but Labour could succeed Conservative, and Conservative then succeed Labour, in such a county as Lancashire with no more ideological clamour than, say, the succession of Wilson by Callaghan. In some areas one party has held control since the advent of universal suffrage. In others, cleavages of opinion developed and the rate of development of comprehensive education was certainly affected by the first arrival of Conservative politicians in power in urban areas in the 1965 local elections. Elsewhere, in Southampton, for example, the same issue took a very long time to become important, whichever party was in power. In the late 1960s much changed in this respect. Local government generally became more contentious and vital. Labour's old guards in London, for example, were forced out in the mid-1960 elections following local government reorganisation and new, and younger, Conservative groups took control. This happened within a less stable national environment in which neither party, after thirteen years of unbroken Conservative rule, could be certain of power for long.

Other changes in local politics followed the 1964 General Election and return of the Labour Government. The bi-partisan gradualism on the issue of secondary education was broken by Anthony Crosland's circular 10/65 which requested all local authorities to make their schools comprehensive. Wholesale reorganisation, and local and patchy resistance to it, became the centre of contention in local government. For the first time, some local authorities openly defied central government. For the first time, as we have seen, central government had to assert itself through the courts in the face of a dissenting local authority. These outbursts of parental and local authority feelings followed the deep anxiety and concern of parents that their children should have a good education. They also demonstrate where, at present, so much of the power lies. For an essential point about the development of educational policy is that whilst many of the main issues have been clarified and determined at the centre, as with the decisions to expand the higher education system and to confirm existing developments by creating the binary system, many policies and practices have developed in the schools and the local education authorities. The comprehensive school was created by local education authorities and most particularly the mainly Labour-controlled councils of Middlesex, London, Birmingham and Manchester, together with some Conservative rural areas who thought them to be the only viable manner of providing secondary education for all. The role of the centre was mainly to confirm or oppose that development and thus it remained until Michael Stewart and Anthony Crosland, Edward Short, Reg Prentice, Fred Mulley and Shirley Williams took up the locally sponsored movement and made it a positive central government policy.

Other areas of development, too, can be ascribed to local rather than central government. Curriculum and educational change are the resultant of many forces—individual teachers working in schools, local and central inspectors and advisers and local administrators, and central government mainly operating through HMIs. It is, however, the head and the teaching staff of the school who decide such issues as whether instruction will be 'formal', that is, concerned with teaching pre-structured concepts, knowledge and techniques to pupils; or 'informal', concerned with promoting learning by exciting children's interest in knowledge which they help to discover or generate.

Thus the development of the British primary school (see Chapter 3) derived from a take-up of the progressive educational theories of Dewey, Froebel and Montessori and mediated through the colleges of education, the advisory and inspectorial network, but starting in practice with individual teachers such as Sybil Marshall in her village school in Cambridgeshire. The schools of the mining villages of the West Riding of Yorkshire, the nursery schools in both the central and the more decorous parts of Bristol, Leicestershire and Hertfordshire, and some of the schools of deeply urban parts of London, may be particularised as places where this important movement of policy and sentiment began.

Because educational policy-making is thus widely distributed among the four levels of the centre, local government, the school and the individual teacher its politics are difficult to comprehend as compared to, say, the politics of North Sea Oil, or of the East of Suez defence policy, or penal policy. An individual school or an individual local authority can create a development that holds true for itself and may or may not become part of a national pattern. Equally, while the centre can promulgate a 'policy' or inaugurate what it hopes may be a national debate about education, it finds it difficult to do so on those issues which touch on the heart of education, the teaching and learning process, and the relationships that lie closest to it.

There is thus an intellectual problem in our subject. Where does the centre take information and concepts for its creation of policy? Does it aggregate the best knowledge and thinking from the main institutions, some 30,000 schools and colleges and 104 local education authorities, or does it start with assumptions and knowledge of its own, derived from 'national' feelings mediated first by MPs and by some of the central interest groups? Does it draw its policies from the political parties of which ministers and opposition leaders are chieftains? Or from the press? Or from research?

The answer is, of course, that the centre makes policies from an amalgam of all of the ingredients but first and last education is a process of teachers communicating with pupils. There is no system, other than some that might be invented to be administered totally by computers, in which the centre can simply make up its mind and then promulgate disaggregated chunks of policy to the system. It cannot realistically aggregate much or most of what goes on in the schools and local authorities. No power on earth can make a true summation of all the discretion enjoyed by all of the teachers within the system. There are national policies. But by the same token there are local authority policies which the national do not subsume. By the same token politics at the even more local level, of the school and the community, take on a life of their own, even though universal political issues emerge. To these more local themes we now return.

The Politics of the School and the Community

As we have seen, the William Tyndale case highlighted issues illustrating virtually every aspect of politics and government of education. Education is a difficult process involving a combination of artistry, human sympathy and knowledge on the part of teachers which, they would argue, means that they need professional freedom. For it is not easy to prescribe the intimacies of interpersonal relationships between teachers and their pupils. This assumption in turn entails the thought that teachers' work should be under teachers' control, as is certainly the case with lawyers, doctors, engineers and architects, although some publicly employed members of these professions work within hierarchies. That was essentially the claim of Terry Ellis, Brian Hadow and their colleagues at William Tyndale School. But that same case also demonstrated how education is value-saturated and that the values of teachers are not the only or even the predominant ones that matter. Education is concerned with learning ways of behaving, of relating to other people, and of learning to construe the rights and duties of the individual in relationship to the wider society and the economy. Many other groups in the society take a view on those issues, and they certainly cannot be restricted to the domain of the teaching profession.

There are, therefore, potential conflicts between teachers' views of how children develop and those of parents and the local authority, which theoretically represents the larger community, the employment system, those who recruit students for higher education, those who are concerned with the resourcing and policing of our society, and many others.

How are people beginning to define these respective roles? The teacher is seen as somebody who is licensed to interpret social needs in the light of his expert knowledge of how children develop and can learn. He is the full-time professional with authority to interpret values as well as to construct processes of skill and knowledge learning. But the teacher has to reckon with others who have an authoritative place in the statement of values and they include their own hierarchies (see Chapter 5) and managers and governors. Managers and governors have an allocated role in the curriculum which is not to make it, but to monitor, test and seek to influence it. Such groups as the Programme for Reform in Secondary Education and the Taylor Committee on the Government of Schools have tried to face the question of how teachers can be free to do their work creatively, free to express their own values, but at the same time be accountable to the governing mechanisms. The answer should be one of fruitful interplay in which the tensions of different ideas and ideologies are reconciled by concession, by explicit statements of what is intended and not by the type of coercion implicit in the actions of the individual teachers at William Tyndale. If there is dispute, the matter can be referred to the local education authority and they must not, the lesson of William Tyndale reads, shirk their duty to resolve conflicts, and to state an overriding view.

These assumptions, that teachers need freedom but are ultimately accountable to local authorities, in the first instance through governing bodies, are classic in the British system but like all else are under severe test now.

The Taylor Committee (1977) struggled with these issues and produced an optimistic formula which assumed that these conflicts can be resolved by power-sharing between the local authority, the teachers, the parents and representatives of the community, all of whom would have equal representation on the governing body. The governing body would set the schools' objectives and have greater financial power than that hitherto delegated to it. This consensual model does not adequately account for the particular roles of each group that it attempts to bring into 'partnership'. Should teachers join in the government of the school where they are employed? Is it a professional or a lay task to create educational objectives? How much independence from the elected local council is desirable? The report responded eagerly to the participation doctrines of its times without too much pause for analysis.

Writing about these issues in 1950 or 1930 we could have virtually forgotten the views of pupils. How hazardous that would be now. Few parts of the country have allowed pupils to become governors and managers and it is, indeed, thought to be illegal for them to figure on a governing body as a member under the age of eighteen. Yet they are the prime clientele of the schools. Moreover, teachers, in reading social values and in interpreting the way that pupils develop must surely need feedback more than token encounters as to how their work is being received by pupils. In higher education, the policy has become constitutional and accepted that students ought to participate in decision-making on academic matters because they have a distinctive contribution to make. Only they can evaluate in a convergent way the total educational experience, for example. They are on course boards, faculty boards and sometimes on senates and council. There have not been, for obvious reasons, equivalent developments in the secondary schools although a pressure group, the National Union of School Students, are seeking to gain membership of governing bodies.

Perhaps the problem is more fundamental than that of institutional formats. There is very little work on the role of the pupil so that teachers and others providing schooling are not clear as to what his expectations of school life are. The way in which teachers create curriculum, through meetings, committee or through hierarchy, may not always take account of the ways in which pupils respond to the work they are already doing.

It would be comforting and intellectually satisfying to be able to make clear generalisations about the relationships between local politics and the development of educational policy. Our problem is that whilst it is possible to state potential contributions to policy development, it is virtually impossible to say how they interact. So far, the reader will have observed, we have referred to several components of local politics that affect educational change. There is first of all the authority and power vested in individual teachers and the schools. The head and his staff cannot easily be controlled or manipulated within our system, and the William Tyndale episode demonstrates not so much the control of the public over schools as the enormous difficulties in securing that control. But, to put that matter into more positive terms, the freedom of the schools is also the reason why we do not have stereotyped and mechanistic education but the possibility at least of creative work deriving from a perception of pupils' needs.

Secondly, however, teacher power at the school level is

increasingly tested by the aspirations and demands of parents and, in some cases, pupils. Parental interest and power has been greatly enhanced and articulated since the early 1960s when such bodies as the Confederation for the Advancement of State Education and the Advisory Centre for Education (see page 133 later) began to make the case for parents' rights of participation in schooling. They, and the National Association of Governors and Managers of Schools, have just secured their most notable victory in the recommendations of the Taylor Committee on the Government of Schools which say that a quarter of the membership of governing bodies should be appointed by parental ballot. As we have seen, there is room for both support and conflict between teachers and parents at the school level. And, to some extent, educational policy will be created by some of those conflicts and collaborations. We then have the relationship between individual schools, teachers and heads and their local education authorities. It must be said, however, that it is rare for conflict to develop on *educational* issues. Conflict has largely been about teachers' conditions of work or the deceleration of the expansion of the education service. Teacher militancy has largely been concerned with resisting cuts made in education by some local authorities, or national salary settlements, or a few cases of teacher discipline. Even when teachers have dissented most strongly on an educational policy, such as the undoubted dislike of many teachers in Tameside for the changes made by the newly appointed Conservative council in 1975, teacher power has not been used. Yet the interaction between teachers and their local authority administrators, inspectors and advisers, and councillors have made indirect but important impacts on the development of educational policy. No one who has witnessed the powerful cultural and social networks established within some local education authorities where, for example, primary education was changing its ways in the 1940s and 1950s can fail to have seen how policy was being made by the sanctioning and encouragement of progressive educational practices.

If, then, the teachers, schools and local authorities interact through patterns of conflict and collaboration so as to change or confirm educational practices, there is then the problem of how those local interactions become part of the national educational scene. We have already indicated that local patterns may well be adopted nationally and that on certain issues the national imprimatur confirms policy. But it is not possible to be certain as to how national policy itself is formed. As we shall see later, the local authority and teacher associations cannot, for good structural reasons, be the principal proponents of change. The DES and the inspectorate will, over time, pick up and perhaps precipitate changes that are occurring locally or that are emerging from its network of relationships with local authorities and with schools. Thus, the plans for the binary system were decisively made at the centre, but were also part of a long tradition of local authorities' desires to retain control over a major segment of higher education. The comprehensive schools were finally installed as a unitary national policy by ministers, but their origins derive from the work of local authorities who for many years had to force the policy against DES resistance.

Thus we can see several points at which educational policy-making is tested, formulated and advanced. It is not possible, however, to see an automatic and easy correspondence between the politics of the community, the workings of local authorities and the formation of national policies. But that uncertainty may well hold of any public system in which there are very many institutions with power to work in their own ways and to form their own relationships with their clienteles. The relationship between central and local policies is not linear but episodic and uncertain.

II: DIFFERENT INTEREST GROUPS

The local authorities and schools are powerful elements in the system. In them resides the power of 400,000 teachers and some 30,000 institutions. We have already raised the question of how they impress their power on the national system and will return to that theme later when looking at central government. From an entirely different standpoint, however, powerful interest groups affect education. Indeed, if we were to compare education with, for example, social work, or health, or housing, we would surely remark how education has a far more clamant set of groups, and a surrounding intelligentsia and press, which have built up strongly over the last fifteen years. Some are of a very long standing and are virtually part of the decision-making system. Others have emerged more strikingly in recent years.

Of the main interest groups, some are all but part of the decision-making system to the point where they have legal or conventional rights to be consulted about policy changes. Such bodies as the Association of Metropolitan Authorities, the County Councils Association, the National Union of Teachers, the National Association of School Masters, the Joint Four Secondary Associations, the Association of Teachers in Higher and Further Education, the Committee of Vice-Chancellors and Principals, are all 'legitimated' and are in the system. They have a 'promotional' purpose in that they are concerned with promoting educational advance. They also have a 'sectional' purpose in that they advance the particular claims of their own members for resources and, where appropriate, as with the teacher associations, for better conditions of work.

The way in which interest groups work is a fascinating area in its own right. Those which are the more powerful because of large membership and a wide span of interest seem inevitably to run the danger of mirroring the organisations upon which they seek to put pressure. The organisation of, say, the National Union of Teachers or the Association of Metropolitan Authorities is smaller, of course, than that of the DES, but its divisional structure, its shadowing of issues by its senior officials, the longstanding employment of very many of them, make it not far different in style, if different in purpose, from that of a public service organisation. This is not surprising or reprehensible but it may account for the ease with which dissident and fringe groups appeal to discontented members.

A further characteristic that divides the interest groups is their internal problems of reaching consensus. The National Union of Teachers has been unfairly criticised as being cumbersome in taking up positions on key issues of policy but it could not move on, for example, comprehensive education, until 1965 for the simple reason that some of its members taught in grammar schools and so massive a teachers' association was quite likely to have the full range of teacher opinion within it, and not all teachers favoured comprehensive schools at that time. Similarly, an examination undertaken of two of the principal local authority associations' confidential committee minutes showed that they mainly reacted to policy issues from the DES and did not initiate discussions on such matters as the creation of the binary system of higher education or the creation of comprehensive schools. Instead, they were naturally concerned with the relationship between the centre and local authorities, teachers' salaries and the flow of resources from central government to their members. The reason was, obviously, that they also had to cater for a wide range of political beliefs among their members and taking a lead on 'education' policies rather than those of resource and overall structure was not feasible. There are indications that such problems as treating severe problems of urban education will begin to engage their attention and that a more developmental mode might prevail.

In contrast to the larger and more strongly established

associations, groups that have been prepared to take a more sectional or particular viewpoint have been able to take a lead, and in a period where more militant attitudes have seemed more in tune with the times. The National Association of School Masters, for example, which for a long time opposed equal pay for women teachers, rapidly increased in membership when it broke the tradition of many decades by bringing its members out on strike in a demand for more pay in 1961. It has become considerably more conformist now, although it takes a particularly trenchant line on such questions as discipline in schools and the need for more legal support for teachers in coping with disruption. An even more striking example, however, of a legitimated but activist and radical union, is the National Union of Students. Apart from the fact that students are in no sense party to the management of education, as all teachers willy-nilly are, the NUS has the particular advantage from a tactical point of view of having an extremely narrow range of political attitudes that are presented on its National Executive. It has moved from being middle-of-the-road social democratic to being 'broad left', a range of political opinion from left-wing Labour to Communist Party, with serious bids for power coming not from the right, but from the extreme left.

In the 1960s the National Union of Students became deliberately politicised, under the leadership of Jack Straw, a centre-of-the-road social democrat. Students demanded the right not only to spend a great deal on union activity, which is financed indirectly from public funds because local authorities must pay the union dues of students to whom they give other forms of grant, but also on general political issues such as apartheid in S. Africa, oppression of civil liberties in Chile, salaries and wages policy, and the miners' strike of 1974. Since Jack Straw's day the NUS has been under the domination of a 'broad left' coalition. But other more extreme left-wing groups have also had a strong influence over policies. Observers at NUS conferences find it impossible to believe that the elected leadership is truly representative of anything like the full range of student opinion which is probably left of centre but contains the whole range of opinions including strong Conservative and Liberal groups in the universities and polytechnics themselves.

The NUS have, however, simultaneously become respectable. They are consulted on student grants. They possess considerable expertise and have been able to tell the DES what some of the issues and data are. They are consulted by ministers on such matters as student representation on the governing bodies of further, higher and college of education governing boards. They have become national figures who are both part-establishment and part of the radical element of British politics.

An earlier generation of change can be called middle-class and parental. The Confederation for the Advancement of State Education, the Advisory Centre for Education, the National Association of Governors and Managers have all become increasingly part of the respectable range of pressure groups although with no formal representative rights to be represented or consulted. Yet they affected the climate of education quite importantly in the 1960s. They expressed middle-class support for the public system of education. They mainly pitted themselves behind progressive modes of education and they asserted the rights of parents to participate actively in the schools, although always moderate in the way in which they lodged their claims. Indeed these interest groups can claim credit for the movement of policy which after some fifteen or sixteen years led to the recommendations of the Taylor Committee that parents should take a quarter of places on governing bodies. They, too, have contributed to the thinking that curriculum, if ultimately determined by teachers, is not their sole preserve. Such a journal as *Where*—produced by the Advisory Centre for Education—has bombarded parents with advice on how to participate in their children's education and assert their rights.

The Media

In part, all of these changes have been both created and reflected by the growth of media interest in education. Before Sir David Eccles became Minister for Education in 1955, there was only one press officer in the DES. There is now a large information division. There is no national newspaper that does not have at least one education correspondent and some provincials have full-timers as well. At least fifty full-time educational journalists are employed, and they form an intimate and close network. *The Times Educational Supplement* and *The Times Higher Education Supplement* are the only *Times* newspapers to make a profit and the *TES* reputedly is the salvation of an otherwise potentially bankrupt newspaper group. Edward Boyle complained in 1971 that the educational press made the news rather than reported it. There is strong and serious interplay between them and the politicians and the academic intelligentsia who pontificate on educational matters and are active in espousing educational causes. As education has become more political and partisan, it has become better news, of course.

DES Responses to Pressure

The DES has been sharply criticised for not being participative enough. It is possible, however, to have sympathy with the Permanent Secretary who asked the Select Committee to say how the DES could be more participative. It had already consulted the legitimate interest groups more than many outsiders would think necessary to be truly democratic. The problem of how a central authority can be in touch with all of the movements and feelings of the institutions it helps to govern is a difficult one.

In the past, the education service has been unusual in the larger number of advisory councils and committees that have fed ideas and feelings into policy-making. The role of such bodies as the Newsom, Robbins, Plowden, Crowther, James Committees have been important but not specific. They have often dealt with very large segments of the education service and their recommendations can be picked up, or disregarded, by government at will. Where the case for change was already recognised, as with the expansion of higher education, reports stood a good chance of being accepted quickly and effectively.

These bodies all had a strong professional and consensual flavour. In recent years, more independent members began to be appointed but this went into sharp reversal after the Plowden Committee on Primary Education was disbanded. The James Committee on Teacher Education and the Oakes Committee on the Management of Further Education were largely composed of professional members from a strictly representative base. Anthony Crosland in 1971 did not conceal his belief that there were 'other ways' in which government could do its long-term thinking. It should improve its own planning and not depend on advisory councils for its thinking. But since then there has been discontent at the way in which the recently created planning system within the DES seems to feed on its own expertise and knowledge rather than bring in wider circles of expertise and values.

The interest groups in education are, perhaps, somewhat different from interest groups in, say, housing or income support and poverty issues. Much of the current policy on supplementary benefits, for example, has been influenced by such groups as the Child Poverty Action Group and housing policy tested by Shelter. By contrast, however, education has so elaborate and varied a formal system of its own that, inevitably, many of the initiatives for change have come from within.

Why should this be so? Some of the reasons have been given. Education has many strong decision- and policy-creating centres—the schools and colleges have styles and continuities of their own. They have, too, the extremely strong network of advisers and inspectors (some 500 HMIs and perhaps 2500 local authority advisers) who constitute a sort of echo chamber within which the teaching profession can test the tones of its own messages. The advisory councils, too, were not adversarial to the education service. They did not provide a counter analysis. Instead they picked up the best practice of the education service and proposed advances which largely built on what had already become clearly desirable to many within education itself. Only perhaps the Robbins Committee radically altered existing policy.

The education service does, indeed, seem to be somewhat different from other comparable areas. The DHSS and its health and social services do not have the same ability to project from the views of its main professions and client groups. There is no equivalent of the 'partnership' of local authorities, teachers and central departments which has often been wrongly (because partnership assumes equality) attributed to education.

This brings us to the way in which the social science intelligentsia, aided and promulgated by the media, pressed on politicians and on government more generally the need for changes, particularly in areas of egalitarian policies and wider participation.

Some of this history has been recounted earlier. The psychologists backed up the 'soft' concept of equality by making 11+ testing feasible. They then joined the sociologists who demonstrated that the advantaged benefited from 'fair' selection systems because they knew how to win competitive games and to benefit from public services. At about the same time psychologists were showing that predictions about children's performance were likely to be unfair to an important minority of them. The economists, in demonstrating the relationship between education and economic growth in the Crowther and Robbins Reports, for example, were exceptionally important in justifying educational expansion. Their present uncertainties on this contribute to the difficulty of justifying more than the present 'steady state' policies in education. Other areas, too, such as social administration, social psychology and sociology all contributed to the questioning of the authority of the public systems. It was they who showed how systems intended to be beneficial may easily label the recipients of benefits. They may be unrepresentative of what the inarticulate want. They may mirror the existing power structure rather than the unexpressed needs of the many.

It could be argued, indeed, that the history of social science interest since 1945 is remarkably near the changing history of the education service. But it would also be easy to overdo the point. Analysts tend to look for change whereas continuity and conservatism most usually predominate. The institutional continuities are still there and the professional power of teachers is still massively strong. But they, too, are affected by the theory and ethos of their times and no period in intellectual history and politics has been so turbulent in the flow of critique and dissent which beneficent bureaucracies and the caring professions have had to face.

III: THE CENTRAL AUTHORITIES

The Department of Education and Science, led by the Secretary of State and its junior ministers, together with its senior permanent officers, works within the parliamentary and more general political environment.

We have already seen how the largest shift in policy has been that of movement from a pluralistic, detached, even agnostic view, towards becoming more directive and committed in its policies, as in the intention to assess educational performance and to establish guidance on a common curriculum through the Assessment of Performance Unit. The Green Paper published by Shirley Williams and John Morris (her Welsh counterpart) in 1977 indirectly expresses the centre's change of role. After organising a large number

137

of conferences throughout the country at which they heard the largely expected views of the main groups in education the government proposed that a review of curriculum arrangements should be carried out by each local authority, to be followed by a broad agreement with the teachers and authorities on a framework for the curriculum, 'and on whether parts of the curriculum should be protected because there are aims common to all schools and pupils at certain stages. These aims must include the achievement of basic literacy and numeracy at the primary stage.' This could hardly be called rampant statism, but certainly moves beyond the earlier assumptions most strongly stated by the centre: that curriculum best derives from pupils' wants and needs as created in the schools. The Green Paper did not say that the DES would prescribe but that it would take a lead in collecting and translating best practices.

The same mood is reflected, but to a lesser extent, in non-curriculum matters. Education, together with the great bulk of local government expenditure, ceased to be subsidised by central government through specific percentage grants. After 1958, a local government act which purported to give local authorities more freedom provided for government monies to reach local government through a general grant. This would be computed in relation to government policies and handed out on objectively determined general needs rather than on specific government approvals and specific local government expenditure. This generalist financial freedom was paralleled in other aspects of central-local government relations. For example, the exceedingly successful moves forward in school building, where economy went hand in hand with good design, encouraged local authorities to develop excellent architectural styles and the DES took pride in the fact that it set minimum standards and maximum cost limits but left local authorities to determine the style and general functional assumptions of the building. Instead of obsessive central control, the ministry tried influence, example and encouragement and created a Development

Group which gave advice on design and cost and also showed how it was possible to be experimental within ministry cost limits. The Development Group in fact worked as if they were private architects for local authorities who opted for their help.

But the doctrine of local and institutional freedom has been tested by the sharp new problems that faced the education service in the 1960s and 1970s. Freedom for teachers to create their own curriculum, for governors of voluntary aided schools to admit pupils on their own principles of selection, for local authorities to spend public money from rates and taxes as long as minimum standards were observed, were doctrines that worked well until a new view of the nature of education policy prevailed. Once the cries for positive measures towards equality were heard, and once public concern about educational standards became expressed, so the issue of teacher freedom became merged with that of teacher accountability. And once the Arabs quadrupled the price of crude oil in as many months, the DES could no longer allow local authorities to act within the margin of financial discretion implied by the general grant. Nor, as we have seen, were the universities allowed their five-year stints of freedom. As I write, the role of central government is being sharpened, although, as we shall see, educational institutions are not easily subordinated to over-arching central policies, particularly since the DES and HM Inspectorate would be reluctant to take centralisation too far.

If we take some of the issues already discussed, we can ask how far did the demands for change come from national institutions. Who made these policies? Theoretically, the prime movers should have included parliament, the Prime Minister, the Cabinet, the Ministers of Education, the national all-purpose interest groups such as the CBI, the TUC and the denominations, and, within the education service, the main educational interest groups representing local education authorities, teachers, parents, students, the many irregulars, such as CASE, ACE, STOPP, NAGM, NSA as well as the intelligentsia and the press surrounding education. It would be naive to assume that any has a clear and certain role in policy generation but, as we shall see, those of whom authority might be expected are less powerful than might be supposed.

Parliament

The role of parliament in policy-making cannot be related in detail here but the author recently studied the extent to which parliament created, affected, and reacted to educational policy-making. The conclusions of that study (1974) were that MPs do less to initiate than to react to policies. In this, again, education reflected the commonplaces of politics as a whole.

The author analysed parliamentary questions and questioned MPs and former ministers about them. Our analysis of PQs from 1960–73 in which we aggregated the numbers on each main subject during the period showed that there was no obvious, significant correspondence between policy generation as represented by a check-list of thirty-five policy areas in education, and the 8000 parliamentary questions asked during the period (for England and Wales only). More important, however, on each of the main issues of the time, as signalled by a ministerial statement or circular, there was no significant grouping of questions, no true reflection of change in intensity of parliamentary interest. Questions rarely preceded change and therefore could hardly have created it, and the subjects barely coincided. In 1960, for example, Labour MPs did not ask PQs about comprehensive schools, or assert the need for an expansion of higher education. MPs mainly used PQs to advance the wellbeing of their constituents which is certainly one legitimate function of parliamentary activity. In 1968, comprehensive schools and fees for overseas students were key issues in education. But the national move towards comprehensive schools did not emerge in PQs. Out of sixty-six PQs on comprehensive schools, forty-three were concerned with local plans, buildings and lack of amenities. In only nine out of twenty-six of the policy areas between 1964 and 1971 was there some correspondence between policy statements and PQs asked. In most, however, no such correspondence can be remarked.

There is no systematic relationship between parliamentary activity and the formation of policies. But MPs still aggregate local interests and anxieties and so keep issues on the educational agenda, if unsystematically. They may bring up a continuous procession of local items which help quicken ministerial interest in the workings of the service which they govern. They cause ministers to exercise more powerful 'management by exception' within their own departments. Ministers tend to listen to their own backbenchers, even if parliament is not as important to them as other influences. But it was difficult to see, from the evidence, any strong temporal or causal links between policy activation and parliamentary activity.

The true focus of parliamentary activity is critique and review and the study reinforced the assumption that the select committees, and the Public Accounts Committee, seemed potentially most important if only because the process they adopt is more exhaustive and overt. But they, too, do not systematically look at educational policies. They take a subject over the quite brief parliamentary year and then drop it. They do, however, enable officials to be questioned by MPs, and interest groups to place their views on the record. It is difficult to find, however, many examples where they had any clear effect in terms of specific responses from government. Some examples can be noted. It is certain that the Albermarle Committee on the Youth Service (1965) which led to expansion and changes in that service, and the training of youth leaders, was the result of a critical Select Committee report published in 1958. Ministers, too, were reinforced in their attitude towards the universities when the Public Accounts Committee investigated the possibility of the audit of universities. This led to a more general discussion of what constituted academic freedom (1966) within a publicly funded system. The report of a Select Committee on race relations (1974) was perhaps less trenchant, and its recommendations less certain but it, too, helped to record some of the changing perceptions about the way in which immigrant school children should be treated. More recently, however, we have had the quite particular episode of a Select Committee investigating policy-making in the DES itself.

The author must be forgiven for pausing a little longer on this last episode, for the report 'Policy Making in the DES' (1976) is important, not so much for its particular conclusions, many of which are perhaps technical in that they tackle the internal machinery and modus operandi of the DES, but for the feelings and more general beliefs that it expressed.

The reader should recall what happened at the Select Committee. An adverse report on the DES by examiners appointed by the Organisation for Economic Co-operation and Development (OECD) triggered it off. The very act of setting up an inquiry demonstrated MPs' awareness of public concern, although that concern was itself boosted by a press scoop of the report before publication. They expressed their concern more explicitly by inviting particular forms of evidence, as well as receiving unsolicited evidence. Their report demonstrated that education is part of general politics. The ways in which the department makes policy; the extent to which civil servants consult and participate with the main interest groups; the extent to which they relate and can relate to wider and client feelings and opinions; the impact that science and the intelligentsia have on policy-making. These issues all came up in evidence and were discussed in the report.

What came out of the report, though it was not said, is that politics in this country are strongly expressed outside as well as inside the legitimised organs of opinion, such as parliament and local government, and the reason for this more vocal expression through the press and media is that parliament is too weak. MPs are given no real power to create policies. Their power to veto is weak because even in the committee system they cannot directly affect the decisions that are ultimately made by the government. Few amendments get through unless they are supported by the government.

The number of changes in major policy forced by member opinion since 1945 can be counted on the fingers of one hand. In these exceptional years of minority government individual MPs have been able to frustrate the Chancellor of the Exchequer's plans to change income tax allowances, or the tax on petrol. But other interventions by individual members have often been in the fields of penal reform and individual rights. For example, the abolition of capital punishment, divorce law reform, abortion and homosexual practices law reform.

Until members have the right to challenge budgetary provisions which they have in form but not in substance, and to make government departments explain what their policies are and why they do not react to suggestions on them, MPs will have no real place in decision-making. The parliamentary study of the DES was briefly dismissed in a departmental reply, and no action on its recommendations taken.

The dangers of giving MPs a stronger part to play can be seen from the American system where legislature is so strong that departments have had to plead, explain their proposals and persuade year by year. Lobbying by constituency and other sectional interests is rife and the bureaucracy too submissive. There is no need to go that far. The DES could be allowed to get on with its decision-making but defend policies in advance and explain more detailed actions, if necessary, in retrospect. Education does seem less subject to political scrutiny than many other zones of public policy although the problem of parliamentary control is a general one.

Education has never in this country seized the politicians

143

as being all that important. MPs may have little influence on economic policy or foreign affairs but they are interested in these themes. However, the evidence must be handled carefully. MPs' attendance at debates, for example, or the number of MPs putting down parliamentary questions are no good index. As Crosland remarked:

> But how do you judge? By the number of Parliamentary Questions? The number of debates? . . . I don't know how many full scale debates there were when I was Minister— perhaps six in all. They weren't very well attended, but then few debates in the House of Commons are unless there is a great political row going on. This isn't at all a good index of the degree of interest . . . Parliament . . . spends most time on things that are going wrong or things that are acutely party controversial and education didn't fall into those categories at that time.

Crosland went on to mention that with the social composition of the parliamentary Labour Party changing there was a change in the balance of interest. 'The debate on overseas students' fees was infinitely more crowded and animated than any debate on primary schools. I doubt if this is wholly a good sign.'

An alternative point of view ought to be recorded, however. Edward Boyle, a former Secretary of State, maintained (in 1976) that a minister's ability to cope with educational business on the floor of the House might well affect spending priorities within the government as a whole. He quotes the example of Florence Horsbrugh losing her job in 1955 as Minister of Education because she could not cope on the floor of the House at a time when the Conservative cause was otherwise prospering. David Eccles seized his opportunities most ably but was helped by the general expectation within the parliamentary Conservative Party that a new minister would mean a fresh start. Boyle also argued that individual debates can influence future decisions.

The Macmillan government came out badly from the debate in April 1962 about the decision to reject the advice of the UGC on the rate of university expansion. This, with unease in the party and Cabinet about other matters affecting universities, played a part in bringing about the decisions in 1963 not only to increase university grants in advance of the Robbins Report but also to accept the main Robbins recommendations within twenty-four hours of the publication of the report.

The views of so experienced and able an actor in these events as Edward Boyle must be respected. Parliament does, of course, trigger off some reactions within the Department of Education and Science. The DES is not all that responsive to outer pressures but is more so than is generally believed. In the opinion of one former junior minister, Timothy Raison, parliamentary questions triggered off questioning and action within the DES.

It is, perhaps, a matter of degree and the outsider sees less going on than the insider. In the view of this author, however, having served on the staff of a Select Committee, the power, access and expectations of MPs are simply inadequate for the tasks that are set to them.

If, then, parliament's role is essentially reactive, and it is primarily concerned with influencing rather than deciding, testing rather than developing and criticising, and reviewing rather than creating policies, it might have been thought that the role would become stronger with the advent of a minority government in 1974. Since certain ministers become more chary of backbench revolts, paradoxically, backbenchers find it more inhibiting to come up strongly against their own ministers when the collapse of a government might mean the loss of several marginal seats.

The sub-committee of the House of Commons Expenditure Committee had no illusions about the weakness of its role. It stated somewhat wistfully in 1976 (para 98, XXXIV):

It is ironic that it should have seemed natural that, in

defending its record of consulting interest groups, the DES made no mention of Parliament, the group with the widest range of interests of all. The elected representatives of the people may ask questions of the DES or speak in debates on education but they are never consulted.

Parliament is thus not the place to which we can look as the forum of change in education. The dramatic changes recorded in this book began elsewhere than in the House of Commons though policies might have been affected by individual members in the House.

Ministers

If parliament is weak, ministers can be strong. They at least have no alibis. The notion that innocent and idealist ministers are betrayed in their best beliefs by Machiavellian civil servants is, in fact, silly and untrue. Civil servants will act in default of political leadership. They will not be frightened to say their piece (as both Anthony Crosland and Edward Boyle testified in 1971). But they will defer to clear political leadership.

Of the main policies passed since the war, those that emerged from the consensus of the educational establishment were formidable but at a minimum had to be endorsed, if not initiated, by ministers. The tripartite system of secondary education and the binary system of higher education largely grew in the womb of the department although they were nourished by the support of the consultative committees and reports such as those of the Hadow, Spens and Percy Committees. But the heroic role of the minister on some issues cannot be gainsaid. The expansion of higher education was certainly pressed by many groups. Eccles and Boyle did, however, both promote and advance the policies advocated by the Robbins Committee. Macmillan had responded quickly to suggestions that the Robbins Committee should be set up, and Home made sure the report was accepted on the day of publication.

The decision to request local authorities to prepare plans for comprehensive education was first written by Michael Stewart, and promulgated by Anthony Crosland. The decision to compel local authorities to conform was made by Edward Short and put into effect by Reg Prentice, Fred Mulley and Shirley Williams. The decisions to revoke the policy were taken, in 1970, decisively and quickly, by Margaret Thatcher and equally decisively revoked by Reg Prentice in 1974. The decisions on the timing of raising the school leaving age, and on increasing the teacher education period to three years, were ministerial, though prepared for a long time by officials and advisory committee reports.

To attempt to discover what caused ministers to act is beyond the scope of political science, unless one is a Marxist or an old-fashioned theologian. Policies are created haphazardly and whilst we can see the pressures that might cause change we cannot predict which pressure will cause which change. Some pressures are resisted by conventions, or by overriding social assumptions that are all but part of our structure. Such students of change as Donald Schon (1971) or Ernest House (1974) analyse examples of networks and of different types of agents that promote change or resist it. But patterns are elusive. For example, it is one of the paradoxes of the system that parties in opposition have clearer ideologies, or commitments to large scale change than parties in power. Once in power, a minister must relate to the total system of interest groups, many of whom, in education at least, are anxious to hasten rather than to arrest the death of ideology. The total government machine led by the Treasury favours consistency and coherence rather than idealism and adventure. The government department serving a minister is concerned to sustain gradualism and continuity that take so long to identify and nourish, and put to work. Machines need inertia and friction as well as motive power, if they are to work well and reliably.

As we have seen, a minister is not consistently affected by

MP opinion although he is an important part of a 'conversion' system which picks up, aggregates, articulates and implements feelings of the larger community. But the relationships between input and output are not clear.

The 'outside' political environment does not present ministers with clear measures and consistent pressure and the main forces pressing on ministers are those of the service itself.

How can we explain these attitudes towards education within parliament and the national political environment? The reasons are difficult to discern. Education is important to individual people but lacks political glamour in central government. This is not true in local government where it remains the biggest spender, and since the comprehensive secondary issue has emerged, also the most 'political' except, perhaps, for the sale of council houses.

One reason may be that there has been uniquely in Britain a serious gap between the public education service and the feelings of politicians and social leaders towards it. Look at the choices they themselves have made. Four Prime Ministers in the twentieth century, Lloyd George, MacDonald, Wilson and Callaghan, did not go to a public school. But their own children or grandchildren have repaired that omission of social good sense. The British have taken a divided, some would say divisive, education system for granted. Nor has the political intelligentsia done any differently even when associated with fashionable radical views. Many of the Labour intellectuals who have supported Labour at the national level have children in private schools. Until quite recently this was not a source of embarrassment or even comment. The rest of the establishment, from the Queen downwards, have never chosen the maintained system for their children with the exception of some members of the most recent Labour governments such as Tony Benn and Anthony Crosland.

Consider the difference with France or Sweden. The Napoleonic system of education produced many odd and bad things but it did at least make it clear that the elite part of the system would be national and public. Not only the Ecole Normale and the polys, but also the lycées in France are universally admired for their rigour, if not for their treatment of young people, and have considerable social esteem. They are public institutions. In Sweden, it is regarded as somewhat bizarre to send one's child to a private school, and they are now being abolished by law anyway. The Americans are now experiencing doubts as some of their public schools become intolerably bad but, historically, the common school has provided for the needs of virtually the whole of the population except for those who seek parochial schools for religious reasons. President Jimmy Carter's daughter goes to the local public school while the socialist British Ambassador, the son-in-law of a Labour Prime Minister, sends his children to private schools in Washington.

It is not only the toffee-nosed, or those who do not put their children where their stated principles are, who have abdicated from the problems of educating the majority of their fellow countrymen. Michael Stewart told the author that Aneurin Bevan had no particular interest or belief in the education service. This author can think of no leading politician or trade unionist, other than those who have made education their speciality, who has made a major speech on the purposes and functions of education except for Anthony Crosland who, in his books, analysed the social importance of education.

No former Minister of Education has ever become Prime Minister, although Alec Douglas Home was at one time Scottish Secretary, a position which included the administration of Scottish education. By contrast, the two most recent Swedish social democratic Prime Ministers, in office between them since 1945 have both been Ministers of Education. For the most part, politicians have become Minister of Education either whilst on their way up to greater things or have been politicians of the second or third rank.

Margaret Thatcher might prove to be an exception to this rule. But it is important to note that when she was Secretary of State for Education no one thought it remotely likely that she would soon become Leader of the Conservative Party and, presumably, the next Prime Minister. Indeed, a former Cabinet Minister, Peter Walker, has related how Mr Heath proposed to transfer Mrs Thatcher from being a full Cabinet Minister in charge of a department into becoming a Minister of State in the Department of Trade and Industry. Education is not normally part of the route to the top.

The main pressures for change have come, then, from within the education service, from the intelligentsia that grew up around it in the 1950s, from the press, and from local politics. Indeed, the connection between local and central politics has grown more important in recent years. For example, Edward Boyle and Chris Chataway advised the London Conservatives on the choice of their leader. They were also consulted about the resistance to be put up by authorities opposed to Labour demands for comprehensivisation. Roy Hattersley, when the Opposition spokesman, began building connections with the Labour leaders of education committees of the large cities. And Conservative rebel authorities have been encouraged by Norman St John Stevas in a way not reckoned to be conventional in previous generations.

If it is true, as I have suggested, that there are continuities and consensuses in the government and management of education which are able to persist throughout more general social and political changes, the place of the civil servants and HMIs, as well as of ministers is obviously central.

Yet although the DES is exceedingly powerful within the education service, within the civil service it is regarded as a little separate. It has the appearance of a Vice-Royalty, something akin to the style of the British Raj in India, a prestigious part of the main system but somewhat remote from it.

A study of the careers of twenty-five Permanent Secretaries

(or their equivalents) from data in the Imperial Calendar and *Who's Who* for 1969 showed that social service departments, including education, were a poor springboard for promotions to permanent secretary and, to a smaller extent, to deputy secretary. The predominance of the Treasury and the Cabinet Office as providing candidates for these posts was marked. Even though all departments suffered from the central departments' preference for their own products, the social service departments suffered most. The Prime Minister's private office and the Cabinet Office had twenty-five administrators on its staff and only three came from social service departments. The social services had a smaller number of top dogs anyway. Yet for many years, the order of preference of candidates on open competition for the administrative civil service was the Treasury, the Home Office and Education.

The civil servants in the department have not been in the mainstream of Whitehall. The response of different heads of the civil service has been to introduce permanent secretaries from the outside and some, at least, have taken time, usually until their day of retirement, to understand the issues. It is also true that able people in the DES have become demoralised by a succession of ministers who have not been up to their job or, if they are, are quickly transferred, whilst their official head might do little to stimulate and encourage creative work within the department. At one time, it was a good department in which to work. On arriving at the ministry from the Treasury in 1957 Edward Boyle remarked that the under secretaries were of equal quality to Treasury third (or deputy) secretaries. The department has had a curious history. Great men have worked within it. In recent years it has been demoralised and has not as yet discovered how to play its role. It has simultaneously been accused of being non-participative and yet too captive to its pressure groups, dictatorial but too unclear of its purposes; reactionary but at the same time committed to a soft view of education.

IV: LINKING CENTRAL AND LOCAL GOVERNMENT AND SCHOOLS

In attempting to make sense of the role of central and local authorities, and of their changing place in policy-making, we come back to points previously stated in this book. Education is based on varying concepts held by varying groups. The continuities valued by the professionals and by the institutions interact with social forces, including the changing needs and desires of education's clientele. The potential tension between those who are elected to decide for the people and those who are appointed to provide expertise in this process is classic in politics and government. Britain is a parliamentary democracy and no matter how powerful various professions or bureaucrats or interest groups or intellectuals might be, ultimately policies are sanctioned, developed or vetoed by politicians who can be dismissed from office. That others are exceedingly powerful does not impugn the general axiom that education is ultimately ruled by the elected representatives who derive their power and authority from the ballot box.

It is, however, a commonplace that deriving power from the people and being subject to dismissal by it does not mean that the popular will operates on decisions that are made. In recognition of this fact a second circuit of democracy involving representative systems other than that of the ballot box is being developed through such devices as parliamentary and local government ombudsmen and stronger governing bodies.

If policy is in the hands of the Secretary of State whose appointer, the Prime Minister, and whose power base, the parliamentary majority, are dismissable, and if it is also shared to some degree with local education authorities which are also dismissable, we come to one or two problems. For running a large educational system of some 30,000 institutions in England and Wales with some nine million pupils and students is a complex business not only because it is a lot of work but because, as we have seen from the previous section, there are different standpoints that might be adopted by those involved in the education business.

For example, the permanent secretary to the DES will have to concern himself with the fact that education uses six per cent of all the economy's output and that, like most activities largely dependent on human labour, the costs are likely to rise rather than decline unless a less good service is to be offered. There is no real scope to replace men by machines in, say, a nursery class or a university tutorial. At the same time, he might have to worry about the fact that in spite of massive expenditures on technical education in the 1960s and early 1970s, Britain's economic efficiency seems to be on the decline. He will also have to worry as to how these points can be argued against the Treasury. He turns a different face to chief education officers who are asking for a larger Rate Support Grant and greater freedom for local authorities.

He will have, too, different concerns from those of his Secretary of State although he might be utterly loyal to the policies and wishes of his political masters. He must face the Treasury and his seniors in the civil service department (who might, if he is of exemplary character and some intelligence promote him into one of the top jobs in the Cabinet Office or the Treasury). The Secretary of State will want to keep well politically so that he or she might get the cherished job at the Home Office or the Foreign Office.

If then we take the chairman of the Education Committee and his director of education, they too have multiple but rather different anxieties. They might be simultaneously under pressure from the ratepayers who are just catching up with the 1975 Houghton Committee Report which added £400 million a year, at one go, to the teachers' salary bill, and from parents who are fed up because the schools do not seem to provide all of the facilities that they think their children need. They face the pressure from the Treasury to cut down on costs, or show why not, from parents who think their children are not learning to spell in the primary schools, and from the teachers' associations which maintain that teachers know what and how children should learn. They are also required to manage a system in which the work is done in virtually impenetrable classrooms by individual teachers working with individual children or groups of them.

Education is therefore part of a traditional ballot-box democratic system. The distribution of resources among different claimant groups, accountability for money spent, concern with the quality of service and its efficiency, are dominant issues for democratic management. But within the ballot-box system, the controversies between clients, professionals and the national government rest uneasily resolved.

It will be well to complete this section on the government institutions by bringing together some of the ambivalences that I feel about them.

First, if one believes that education begins and ends in the classroom, it becomes exceedingly difficult to see how national policies such as those for advancing equality or ensuring that the economy receives the trained manpower it needs are devised and carried out. This is part of the larger problem of governability which is exercising some political scientists just now. In some way or the other, central government has to be able to set the framework for progress whilst respecting the organic continuities of education in institutions which have a right to a life of their own. Setting conditions by which others can work creatively is a matter of art as well as of administrative and political science.

Secondly, in this chapter I have pointed out some of the serious democratic weaknesses of the system. Whilst not at all diminishing the point that teachers and schools and local communities need to be able to sort out what they want from education, albeit within a national framework, it becomes searingly important that parliament has more power if the present dreadful downward spiral of MP expectations and performance is not to get worse, and if educational decision-making is to remain at its present somewhat uninspired and unreflective level. If parliament were stronger, the DES would become stronger as well, because it would be required to say more boldly and confidently what it is doing and to defend itself more adequately. At the same time both politics and administration might attract the attention of outside groups who would join in the task of providing a wider range of policy analyses.

Whilst education is not regarded as central to the main issues of politics, it yet demonstrates virtually all of the issues that affect politics. Our interest groups are potent, but they have not the ability of their American counterparts to recognise good and strong political issues when they see them, and to act on them. As an academic, I can also testify to the way in which political scientists too easily go for the 'big game' of their subject—the role of parliament or of the Cabinet, and fail to exploit academically the way in which the perennial issues of political philosophy emerge in our schools and the power structures surrounding them.

Finally, this chapter has been both optimistic and pessimistic. It is optimistic because it has shown that major issues are being taken up at the local level and that they are not always lost in the ephemeral wildnesses of sectional groups. It is an ugly time for those who believe that the public deserves institutions which will serve them well. Disruptive actions, irresponsible claims for salaries, the strident paraphernalia of student bureaucracy and trade union militancy, all leave the ordinary citizen wondering whether his power to elect councillors and MPs can be of avail to him. But here and there, as in the Tyndale, Tameside and Enfield cases, courageous groups, some of them courageous in wrong causes, are showing that it is possible to affect events, by due process. These do not add up however, to affecting the larger policies, and it is to those that I turn in the concluding chapter.

Chapter 11 Future Prospects

The main theme of this book has been the way in which education represents many of the features prevalent in British politics in the 1960s and 1970s. In particular, it has tried to show how a sphere of human activity which affects the great majority of the people has been subject to strong movements of ideology, intellectual fashion and political beliefs which the authorised institutional framework has found it difficult to contain. Education possesses many continuities of policy and institutional systems yet uncertainties about the power of the conventional democratic structure have been most potently advanced in recent years.

Stability can always be overstated. Everything changes, and all the while. Relationships between individuals and groups in the society are forever changing although the last decade has been more volatile than any preceding period except, perhaps, the 1640s. In education, the change agents have been particularly vocal and successful. But such theorists of change as Donald Schon (in his masterly *Beyond the Stable State*, 1971) exaggerate the turmoil to which human beings and their institutions are subject. Education is an institutionalised form of relationships between individuals. The education system is a way in which varying human wants are met by at least a minimally acceptable standard. Because, however, it involves all of the institutional paraphernalia of hierarchy, democratic process, formalised decision-making, rules and procedures, it is subject with particular force to the attacks that have been made on institutionalism. Part of the discourse about education is how discourse itself will be conducted.

So those who wish to consider the future of education will have to determine how far institutionalism is acceptable and essential. They will surely conclude, as all critical minds have concluded in the past, that education is over-institutionalised, that teachers have too much power, that clients do not have enough, and that bureaucracy is prevalent. But they will then experience a more vexing difficulty in deciding what form a less institutionalised system will require. They will have to determine, in particular, how far the demands for change can be reconciled with the needs of individuals. Demands for change are no less collectivist than the systems which they are seeking to change. Has any radical reformer finished up with a system which does not in its turn compel the majority to accept collective procedures? Deinstitutionalising society ˙ is just not on.

Moreover, once reformers have determined what changes are acceptable, and how individual needs will be met in new systems, they will then have to decide how far education itself is an independent system and how far it can take a lead in creating social change. In this book, I have been uncertain as to how far social changes have derived from education or how far educational change is itself merely an expression of wider social changes. Reformers have assumed that education can affect society. They now more cautiously assume that the effects will be felt only if other parts of the social system change at the same time.

A further point for the future is the question of how far changes are, in fact, acceptable. I am not too certain about this. Working-class parents do not like primary school progressivism. Nor have they been the most fervent supporters of comprehensive education. Working-class electors, who stand to be the highest beneficiaries of the expansion of higher education, have not been particularly enthusiastic about the growth of a large student proletariat whose ways of life and aspirations they cannot easily reconcile with their own wishes and working lives. If change means a move towards deinstitutionalising education it is by no means clear that the mass of the people are for it.

But what changes, then, are desired and acceptable? Some

of those discussed in this book concern the attacks on authority, the demand for more participation and the critical analysis of the present governing system. The central government departments have certainly opened up far more than in previous years but by common consent are still far too closed. Educational planning could certainly be far more open, and not exclusively undertaken by civil servants and the idiosyncratically chosen groups of outsiders whom they decide to consult. This does not mean, however, that bureaucracy should become weaker. In my view it should become stronger: strong enough to be able to make public its thinking, to swing with the punches, to stand up to debate and criticism. It can then look for support from those who become more knowledgeable about what is being planned. More important, however, a different political framework seems essential. On this, there are several strands which might be pursued. Some of them concern the ability of the system to be predictive. Others concern the ability of the system to bring in the best thinking to its aid.

Almost all of the changes in this book could not have been predicted fifteen years ago. Speculation about educational futures even in the relatively short term is hazardous. In 1966 no one would have believed that the educational system would now be experiencing an absolute reduction in teacher education places, because of a demographic decline and a reduction of demand expressed as a proportion of those who stay on voluntarily beyond sixteen. Nor could the optimism about the ability of education to create the good life and a sound economy have been expected to be replaced by a dour and often unreflecting pessimism about the effect of education.

In the 1960s it seemed possible to state the aims and purposes of education and to find its means. Instead, as we have seen, sophisticated indeterminacy describes policy process as incremental and disjointed. It rejects rationalistic attempts to predict what people need and to find the means of achieving it.

The educational planner cannot rely on any particular

model of change. He must accept that changes are not linear. No fixed sequence of time and logic as between the different components can be discerned. Within the policy process it is impossible to sort out causes and effects and components can be latent, biding their time for a change of circumstances, or dynamic, or simply never happen. Moreover, there is sedimentation of many of the more important elements. Institutions, curricula, resource distributions, buildings, all represent an accretion of historic commitments which need not be outmoded but which are the result of interaction between components of the past and the potent present.

Policy-makers must therefore be eclectic. They must state as broad a range of the futures as their own imagination and the collated imaginations of others make it possible. They have to accept that social and educational planning has to create à la carte menus in the sure knowledge that consumers will not eat what is provided according to any predictive plan. Certain staples of the diet will remain. But a large margin will be uncertain. And the planner himself is a part of an interactive process which is itself uncertain. That is why the Great Debate on education had a hollow ring. Will mass conferences of worthies enable everybody's needs and feelings to be brought together?

A few certainties will always remain. Parents will want their children to be skilled in arts that enable them to earn a living. The great majority of people will want their children to be taught to conform to the prevailing social norms. The majority will not want to participate in decision-making themselves let alone take part in perpetual folk moots about future policy, but will want a reasonable chance to represent their views to the system. It is, too, a glaring artefact of the education system that it is not like the administration of income tax, or the economy, or British railways or foreign policy because the centre cannot take grip of the main essentials of the education process. Teaching and learning will always develop in the schools, between teachers and taught. The centre can, however, establish the conditions of resources and planning structures within which educational processes take place. It can also help collate more general social views about what teachers are doing and ensure that teachers do not simply continue as if they are accountable to their own consciences and to their own peer groups. It is an issue as to whether the political setting created by governing bodies, rights and duties of teachers, and the rights of parents and pupils, is fully taken into account by central government. The relationship between the centre and the periphery is firmly based on a belief in the power of the periphery. And, to the credit of the British system, that is the established doctrine which now prevails.

The continuities and certainties will probably look after themselves. But how will the system ensure that the moving parts of educational thinking are taken into account? This brings us to the serious problems of the quality of politics in Britain. Enough has already been said in Chapter 10 about the way in which parliament is short of the powers it needs for it to be able to provide an adequate counter analysis to that of the central government department. In local government, the position is far better for councillors are certainly able to influence local policies, and there are good opportunities for able people to move from election as a councillor to positions of power within their own community.

At the national and more general social level, however, this has not been the case. Talented politicians have become ministers but these have been very few. Of the fifteen ministers appointed since 1945, only ten can be said to have been competent enough to occupy any senior office, let alone that of Secretary of State for Education and Science, and some would put the number even lower.

Such movements as the development of higher education and of comprehensive education were the results of creative, thoughtful and committed thinking about what was wrong with the system and how those wrongs might be righted. There is no guarantee that the same level of thinking will go into the next stage of implementing policies. Whilst such figures as R. H. Tawney and the ablest of the psychologists and sociologists developed the general case for reform, no equally able group of politicians and administrators were able to pick up the general social issues and to convert them into policies. Change agents there have been in the schools and local authorities. But reformers on a national scale have been lacking. There is a gap between feeling out of the comprehensive issue by the early seers and its implementation by Fred Mulley and Ashly Brammell.

This points to the need for an action intelligentsia which is as able as are the first pioneers and theorists to get things going. Certainly this has happened in primary education. There the practitioners refuse to be theoretical. They have secured successes which they can no longer easily defend. In secondary education, however, only a few practitioners have been speculative about what ought to happen—Margaret Miles, Margaret Maden, for example—in their own schools, and they have had to rely too much on the sociological and psychological cases against selection. In other words, choices on policies ought to be made partly on assumptions about who will be around to implement them. In other walks of life we would not undertake major exercises without thinking through all of the stages involved. For example, major surgery has to be preceded by careful diagnosis and followed by careful after-care. The creation of a major building involves selection of the site, design of the building and then highly professional engineering and building. We have hardly begun to think about the continuity problem in educational futures.

So two gaping lacunae appear in the intellectual and political environment within which educational policies must move. There is no competent liberal and socialist intelligentsia that is feeding the political system with new concepts about the educational system. Simple notions of equality, of the power of the economy and the planning system to create social good, have faltered and no new clear concept, let alone paradigm, is being fashioned other than the confusingly

161

various notions about participation described on pages 68 and 72.

Moreover, this country seems incapable of identifying, recruiting, promoting and sustaining competent political leadership. The brilliance of educational idealism of the 1930s and 1940s has flickered weakly as it has come to be implemented in the hands of a succession of politicians from both parties who have been at best well meaning and amiable and at the worst, weak or uncaring or opportunistic. For these reasons the author is certain that several things need to happen. The political system must be toughened up so as to create strong non-ministerial roles. That means more power for MPs through the strengthening of the parliamentary committee system and the granting of real facilities to probe, attack, state and propose. Stronger MPs might themselves be able to energise the political system by providing a richer source for the recruitment of ministers and other political leaders and by making the interplay between the executive and the political environment tougher and more real. Reciprocally, however, we need a stronger intelligentsia. British academic life still gives status to the theoretical. Those who wish to concern themselves with public policies must be political and evangelical as well as analytic. The private foundations, the research councils and perhaps even government itself must think through the place of the academic and of the able outsider in the development of policies.

We have been describing a system that has been through terrible problems of resources and uncertainty of purpose. Yet the fabric is still firm. There are still inside groups who run the whole thing. The facts that theories of participation are weak and that the opposition is never any better than the government or that critics often have no real alternative to offer, do not rid us of the disturbing knowledge that consensus was often the least line of resistance rather than the critical path determined analytically.

Short Bibliography

Baron, G. and Howell, D. A., *The Government and Management of Schools* (Athlone Press, 1973)

Boudon, R., *Education, Opportunity and Social Inequality* (Halsted Press, 1972)

Coates, R. D., *Teachers' Unions and Interest Group Politics* (Cambridge University Press, 1972)

Evetts, Julia, *The Sociology of Educational Ideas* (Routledge & Kegan Paul, 1973)

Fowler, G., Morris, V., and Ozga, G. (eds.), *Decision Making in British Education* (Heinemann, 1974)

Gretton, J. and Jackson, M., *Collapse of a School — or a System?* (TES and Allen & Unwin 1976)

House, E. R., *The Politics of Educational Innovation* (McCutchan Publishing Corporation, 1974)

Kogan, M., *Educational Policy Making* (George Allen & Unwin, 1975)

Kogan, M., *The Government of Education* (Macmillan, 1971)

Kogan, M., *The Politics of Education* (Penguin, 1971)

Kogan, M., and Packwood, T., *Advisory Committees and Councils in Education* (Routledge & Kegan Paul, 1974)

Kogan, M. with Van Der Eyken, W., *County Hall* (Penguin, 1973)

Locke, Michael, *Power and Politics in the School System, A Guide Book* (Routledge & Kegan Paul, 1974)

Manzer, R. A., *Teachers and Politics: The Role of the National Union of Teachers in the Making of National Educational Policy in England and Wales Since 1944* (Manchester University Press, 1970)

Parkinson, M., *The Labour Party and the Organization of Secondary Education 1918–1965* (Routledge & Kegan Paul, 1970)

Pateman, T. (ed.), *Counter Course* (Penguin Books, 1973)

Peters, R. S. (ed.), *Perspectives on Plowden* (Routledge & Kegan Paul, 1969)

Short Bibliography

Saran, R., *Policy Making in Secondary Education* (Clarendon Press, 1973)

Searle, John, *The Campus War* (Penguin Books, 1972)

Simon, Brian, *The Politics of Educational Reform, 1920–40* (Lawrence & Wishart, 1974)

OFFICIAL REPORTS

Infant and Nursery Schools (Hadow Report), HMSO, 1933

Secondary Education with Special Reference to Grammar Schools and Technical High Schools (Spens Report), HMSO, 1938

Higher Technological Education (Percy Report), HMSO, 1945

Fifteen to Eighteen (Crowther Report), HMSO, 1959

The Youth Service in England and Wales (Albermarle Report), Cmnd 929, HMSO, 1960

Half our Future (Newsom Report), HMSO, 1963.

Higher Education (Robbins Report), Cmnd 2154, HMSO, 1963

The Government of Colleges of Education (Weaver Report), HMSO, 1966

Children and their Primary Schools (Plowden Report), HMSO, 1967

Teacher Education and Training (James Report), HMSO, 1971

Report of the William Tyndale Junior and Infant Schools Public Inquiry (The Auld Report), ILEA, 1976

A New Partnership for our Schools (Taylor Report), DES and Welsh Office, HMSO, 1977

Education in Schools. A Consultative Document (Green Paper), Cmnd 6869, HMSO, 1977

Tenth Report from the Expenditure Committee, 'Policy Making in the Department of Education and Science', 'Fookes Committee Report), HMSO, 1976

Index

Keywords
Raymond Williams

Alienation, creative, family, media, radical, structural, taste: these are seven of the hundred or so words whose derivation, development and contemporary meaning Raymond Williams explores in this unique study of the language in which we discuss 'culture' and 'Society'.

A series of connecting essays investigating how these 'keywords' have been formed, redefined, confused and reinforced as the historical contexts in which they were applied changed to give us their current meaning and significance.

'This is a book which everyone who is still capable of being educated should read.' Christopher Hill, *New Society*

'. . . for the first time we have some of the materials for constructing a genuinely historical and a genuinely social semantics . . . Williams's book is unique in its kind so far and it provides a model as well as a resource for us all.'
Alasdair MacIntyre, *New Statesman*

'. . . an important book.' F. W. Bateson, *Guardian*

'. . . excellent and penetrating. It must be added to any shelf of reference books about words.' Woodrow Wyatt, *Sunday Times*

Fontana Politics

Fontana Books

Fontana is a leading paperback publisher of fiction and non-fiction, with authors ranging from Alistair MacLean, Agatha Christie and Desmond Bagley to Solzhenitsyn and Pasternak, from Gerald Durrell and Joy Adamson to the famous Modern Masters series.

In addition to a wide-ranging collection of internationally popular writers of fiction, Fontana also has an outstanding reputation for history, natural history, military history, psychology, psychiatry, politics, economics, religion and the social sciences.

All Fontana books are available at your bookshop or newsagent; or can be ordered direct. Just fill in the form and list the titles you want.

_____

FONTANA BOOKS, Cash Sales Department, G.P.O. Box 29, Douglas, Isle of Man, British Isles. Please send purchase price, plus 8p per book. Customers outside the U.K. send purchase price, plus 10p per book. Cheque, postal or money order. No currency.

NAME (Block letters)

_____

ADDRESS

_____

_____

_____